PENGUIN BOOKS

SREBRENICA
RECORD OF A WAR CRIME

Jan Willem Honig was born in 1958 and educated at the University of Amsterdam and King's College, London. He joined the Department of War Studies at King's College in 1993 as a lecturer, after having taught at the University of Utrecht and New York University. He was also a Research Associate at the Institute for East–West Security Studies in New York. He is the author of *Defence Policy in the North Atlantic Alliance: The Case of the Netherlands* (1993).

Norbert Both was born in 1970 in Malawi, his family returning to the Netherlands in 1973. He was educated at the University of Amsterdam. He took an MA in International Studies at the University of Sheffield and graduated with distinction. Between 1994 and 1995 he assisted Lord Owen in the research for his memoirs, *Balkan Odyssey*. He is currently researching Dutch foreign policy regarding the Yugoslav conflict at the University of Sheffield.

"Dramatic, wrenching and horrific . . . [the book] details the final battle for Srebrenica and the murder of its men, it attempts to explain why the Bosnian Serbs committed such a horrific act of genocide, and it analyzes why the international community sleep-walked into the disaster."
— William Shawcross, *The Sunday Times* (London)

"A carefully researched and devastating book . . . [Honig and Both] set out in chilling detail the collapse and subsequent bloodbath at Srebrenica, as well as its terrible ordeal over the previous three years."
— Robert Fisk, *The Independent*

"A fascinating and detailed chronicle"
— Martin Bell, *The Times* (London)

JAN WILLEM HONIG AND
NORBERT BOTH

—————

SREBRENICA

RECORD OF A WAR CRIME

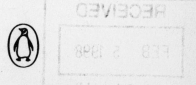

PENGUIN BOOKS

BJY 7520-1/3

PENGUIN BOOKS

Published by the Penguin Group

Books USA Inc., 375 Hudson Street, New York, New York 10014, U.S.A.

Penguin Books Ltd, 27 Wrights Lane, London W8 5TZ, England

Penguin Books Australia Ltd, Ringwood, Victoria, Australia

Books Canada Ltd, 10 Alcorn Avenue, Toronto, Ontario, Canada M4V 3B2

uin Books (N.Z.) Ltd, 182–190 Wairau Road, Auckland 10, New Zealand

guin Books Ltd, Registered Offices: Harmondsworth, Middlesex, England

First published in Penguin Books (U.K.) 1996

Published in Penguin Books (U.S.A.) 1997

1 3 5 7 9 10 8 6 4 2

Copyright © Jan Willem Honig and Norbert Both, 1996

All rights reserved

ISBN 0 14 02.6632 1 (pbk.)

(CIP data available)

Printed in the United States of America

Set in Monotype Bembo

Pessimum facinus auderent pauci, plures vellent,
omnes paterentur.

(The worst crime was dared by a few, willed by more
and tolerated by all)

Tacitus

Contents

Acknowledgements

This book could not have been written without the help of David Owen and James Gow. They believed in the importance of the book's topic and supported us accordingly. BBC *Panorama*'s Jane Corbin, Andrew Williams, Camilla Geddes and Julia Hannis generously provided us with key source material from their 1996 'War Crime' documentary. Margriet Prins of UNHCR Tuzla provided great assistance on the ground in Bosnia. Other people whose help was highly appreciated are: Emina Babović, Mirha Bečirović, Drea Berghorst, Richard Borst, Charlef Brantz, Richard van Duuren, Magda Ferdinandus, Harm Hazewinkel, Charles Lane, André Lommen, David Ludlow, Pascale Meige, Jan van der Meulen, Francisco Otero y Villar, Doke Romeijn, René van Rijckevorsel, Alosman Saletović, Laura Silber, Maggie Smart and Bert Steinmetz.

We thank Ian Kearns, Stephen George and John Hawthorne of the University of Sheffield and Lawrence Freedman of King's College, London, for their patience and moral support. Our editors, Andrew Kidd and Peter Carson, deserve praise for their tough-mindedness with two academics who had an almost incurable tendency to want more time to ponder and ruminate on the subject.

We acknowledge permission from the Trustees of the Liddell Hart Centre for Military Archives at King's College, London, for permission to use the materials from the *Death of Yugoslavia* television series produced by Brian Lapping Associates.

As is inevitable with a book of such a contemporary and in many ways sensitive nature, we are also indebted to many people who prefer not to be mentioned in person. They will know who they are. Any errors in fact and in judgement are solely our responsibility.

We are very grateful to Suzanne and Graciella, who made many sacrifices so that we could write this book.

NOTE TO THE READER

We have used so-called military time indications throughout the book. The designations 'Muslim' and 'Bosnian' are used interchangeably.

Finally, we would like to point out that although both authors have a namesake appearing in the book, this is a matter of pure coincidence. There is no family relationship.

Maps

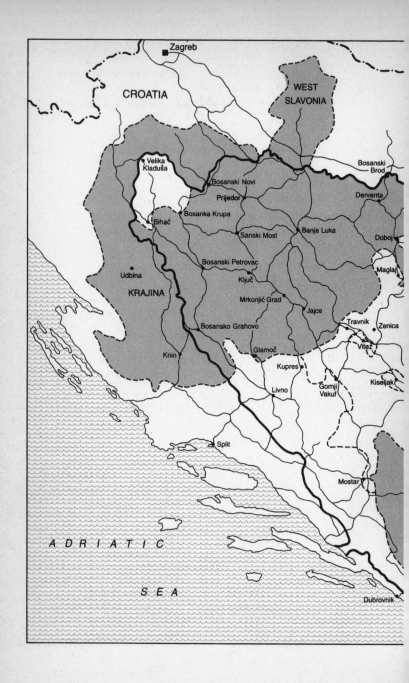

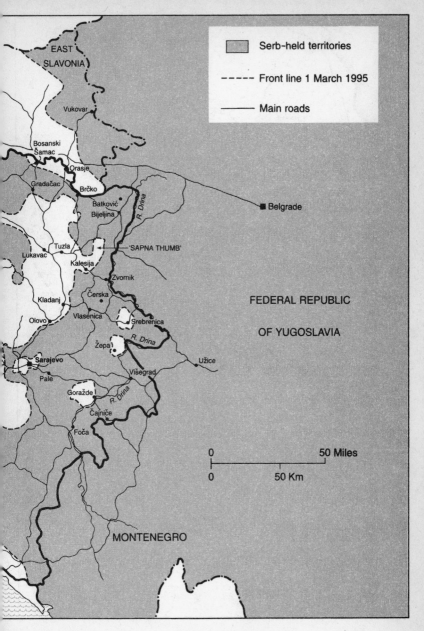

Bosnia — Herzegovina

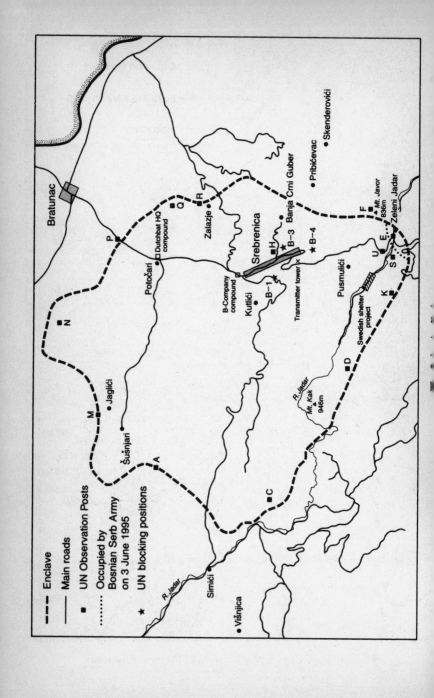

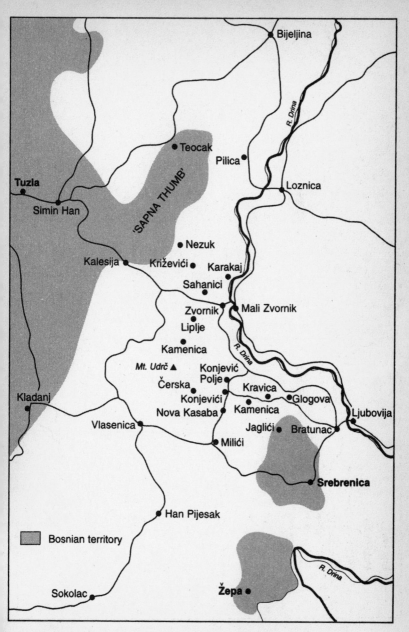

Area of attempted escape route and massacre sites of the Srebrenica men

Introduction

Potočari, Bosnia, 13 July 1995. The road is littered with bags and discarded clothes. Muslim refugees walk alongside a row of buses. Suddenly, they move off the tarmac as an armoured vehicle drives past. They step back on to the road, which runs past what used to be the main camp of the Dutch United Nations peacekeepers in the Srebrenica enclave. The refugees walk on, directed by Serb soldiers and policemen. 'Stop! Come on! Good. Follow then! In a queue! One by one. Left. Move! Move!' The afternoon sun is beating down. The refugees look flushed and exhausted. They have not been able to wash themselves for days and have not drunk and eaten properly for a long time. They do not protest but simply follow orders. The women get into the buses with their children and sit down in silence, their faces blank. The men have not been allowed on to the buses and are still standing by the side of the road.

Some distance away, sacks of belongings and clothes are piling up in the courtyard of a white house. This is where the Muslim men are being assembled and interrogated, before being transported to a separate location from the women. They have been stripped of their personal possessions. The Serb camera filming the scene suddenly captures the face of a Dutch army doctor, Colonel Gerry Kremer. The Serbian cameraman asks Kremer, 'What's going on?' The tense Kremer, his face burnt by the sun, replies: 'You know what is going on. You know . . .'

For two days Kremer and the other Dutch UN 'blue helmets' had watched Muslim men being separated from their families. Most of the Dutch knew they were being forced to witness and even cooperate in an 'ethnic-cleansing' operation. Later, Kremer described the situation as a 'combination of *Schindler's List* and *Sophie's Choice*'. The vast majority of the Muslim men met a gruesome fate. They were executed and anonymously buried in mass graves, many were tortured before being killed, a small number were put in prisons and only very few managed to escape.

While the Serbs were 'evacuating' the Muslim refugees from Potočari, they were also killing and capturing as many men as possible of the 10,000–15,000 who had broken out of the enclave in an attempt to reach Bosnian government-held central Bosnia on foot. Though several thousand of the stronger men, mostly regular soldiers, made it through the Serb lines, the weaker ones were captured in their hundreds. Most of them were executed. By 16 August 1996, the Red Cross had registered 6,546 tracing requests for people missing from Srebrenica, 6,513 of whom were men.

Though the Srebrenica enclave was now exclusively Serb, Muslims had been in a majority before the war began in Spring 1992. The 1990 Yugoslav census stated that out of a population of 36,666 for the whole Srebrenica *opština* (district), 75.2 per cent claimed the Bosnian Muslim nationality. Serbs made up 22.7 per cent. In Srebrenica town itself, a community of some 6,000, the ratio was the same.

The town of Srebrenica lies tucked away in a steep-sloped valley in eastern Bosnia. In better times, its inhabitants did well out of the proceeds from tourism and in the mining and textile industries. The name of the town, which is derived from the word *srebren* ('silver'), indicates its long historical association with the metal, stretching back to Roman times when it was called *Argentaria* ('silvermine'). Srebrenica's relative isolation was an important reason for its survival against the initial Serbian onslaught in Bosnia-Herzegovina in Spring 1992. On the other hand, its proximity to the Drina river and to Serbia proper meant that, ultimately, it would not be able to escape the combined might of the Bosnian Serb and Yugoslav armies.

Except for a few days in April 1992, Muslims remained in control of Srebrenica through three years of war. It became a symbol of Bosnian resistance and was featured in Bosnian pop songs. But on 11 July 1995 the existence of Muslim Srebrenica came to an abrupt end. On that day Bosnian Serb television broadcast an announcement by General Ratko Mladić, the commander of the Bosnian Serb Army. Clearly on a high, the Serb general told television viewers that the moment for revenge against the 'Turks' had finally come. Speaking from 'Serbian Srebrenica' he gave the city as a 'present to the Serb nation'.

With the take-over of Srebrenica, and one week later Žepa, the Serbs controlled a large swath of 'ethnically clean' land in eastern Bosnia, even though between January 1993 and July 1995 successive failed peace plans had always envisaged that Srebrenica and Žepa would remain Muslim towns. Under the ten-province Vance–Owen plan, Srebrenica was to become part of the Muslim-majority Tuzla province. But in April 1993 the Serbs reduced Muslim-held territory around Srebrenica to a small pocket of land containing some 50,000 Muslims. With no foreign government willing to reverse the Serbian military gains in eastern Bosnia, Srebrenica was kept artificially alive for another two years as a small isolated enclave after being declared a 'safe area' by the UN Security Council. Two alternative proposals, the European Union Action Plan of 1993 and the Contact Group map of 1994, envisaged Srebrenica as linked to the two other Muslim enclaves in eastern Bosnia: Žepa and Goražde. But in July 1995 the Serbs took Srebrenica and Žepa and changed the Contact Group map by force. The subsequent US-brokered Dayton Accords of November 1995 accepted this as writ, and Srebrenica and Žepa became part of the Republika Srpska, the Bosnian Serb republic.

The massacre that followed the Serb take-over of Srebrenica must count as the largest single war crime in Europe since the Second World War. Between 6 and 16 July 1995 the Serbs seized the Srebrenica safe area, expelled 23,000 Bosnian Muslim women and children and captured and executed thousands of Muslim men.

This book has three goals. The first is to give a detailed interpretation of the 'battle' for Srebrenica of 6 to 11 July and the deportations and mass executions that followed. The second is to explain why the Bosnian Serbs attacked the Srebrenica safe area and sought systematically to kill so many Muslim men. The third is to analyse why the international community did not prevent these Serb actions.

'Srebrenica' has become synonymous with such an extraordinarily horrific crime that exceptional explanations have been proposed. Stories of conspiracy and betrayal abound. The most popular theory is that Srebrenica fell as the result of a plot involving senior UN personnel, the French government and the Serbian government.

Others place the blame firmly on the Dutch UN soldiers, whom they accuse of cowardice during the Serb offensive against the safe area. We reject these explanations. Conspiracy theories tend to be neatly constructed so that every decision, or failure to decide, seems to stem from sinister ulterior motives. They leave no room for the dilemmas of real life, nor for miscommunication or outright failure. As such they rarely bring us closer to the truth, and more often create a fertile breeding ground for dangerous stab-in-the-back myths.

As for final culpability, this must rest squarely on the shoulders of the most senior Serbian politicians and officers. They authorized and organized the crime. Their responsibility is clearly shown by a careful analysis of the crime, as given in this book. The crime's systematic nature, the indications of extensive planning and carefully followed procedures, all point to the direct responsibility of the Bosnian Serb leadership in Pale and the collusion, at the very least, of the Serbian leadership in Belgrade.

This does not mean, however, that many of the world's 'United Nations' do not deserve strong criticism for what did, and did not, happen. The UN Security Council, the Bosnian government, the five-nations Contact Group and, in particular, the Dutch government never came to terms with, let alone solved, the problems inherent in applying a concept of 'safe areas'. At the heart of these problems lay a moral dilemma. How could one effectively oppose ethnic cleansing and support the creation of safe areas, when one was unwilling to risk the lives of peacekeepers in the process of protecting these safe areas?

The failure of the safe-area policy in the case of Srebrenica was not, as some have claimed, in the first place a failure on the part of the Dutch blue helmets in Srebrenica or the peacekeeping mission in the former Yugoslavia. The senior UN military commanders in the former Yugoslavia, by 1995, were developing a strategy that sought to address realistically the military problems of keeping the UN peace-keeping mission in Yugoslavia alive and also giving the safe areas a chance of success. Rather, as this book argues, the safe-area policy failed because of a contradictory moralistic impulse and a lack of collective will to use (some) force on the part of the international community. Srebrenica's tragedy was that its fate was determined by the Serbs before the 'United Nations' resolved the dilemmas they had created for themselves.

Part One

The Fall of Srebrenica, July 1995

CHAPTER ONE

The Attack

On Saturday 8 July 1995, the Dutch Defence Minister, Joris Voorhoeve, was helping his son move house in Groningen. Far away, in Bosnia, Serb forces were attacking the Muslim enclave of Srebrenica. During the previous two days there had been a significant increase in military activity on the perimeter of the UN Security Council-declared 'safe area'. That Saturday morning, however, the Dutch battalion protecting the area had reported only sporadic firing. Although 'the bunker', the Crisis Management Centre deep under the Ministry of Defence in The Hague, had been on the highest state of alert since Friday, no one believed that the final attack was under way. The judgement of the UN commanders on the ground in the former Yugoslavia was that the incidents of the previous days were acts of 'provocation' and 'intimidation', not the prelude to an all-out offensive. The Minister could take the Saturday off.

Late in the afternoon, Voorhoeve's mobile phone rang. The Minister learnt that a Dutch soldier had just died. A squad of Dutch troops had been forced to abandon their observation post on the southern edge of the enclave after heavy Serb shelling. While retreating, they had run into Bosnian Muslim troops who had thrown a grenade at their armoured vehicle. Private Raviv van Renssen, the gunner, just failed to close his hatch in time and had been hit in the head by shrapnel. Attempts to save his life had failed. He had died at 16.27.

As was his habit with important statements, Voorhoeve personally drew up the public declaration announcing Van Renssen's death. The Minister's military advisers saw the first Dutch combat death in Srebrenica as an isolated incident. The overall situation was not judged serious enough to warrant Voorhoeve's return to The Hague. Yet within a week, the safe area of Srebrenica would no longer exist.

Thousands of Muslim men would be dead, executed by Serb soldiers, and 23,000 women and children deported.

With hindsight, it is clear that the signs were gravely misinterpreted. The Serbs *did* intend to capture Srebrenica, once and for all. The attack was typical of Serb military operations. Serb offensives followed a standard pattern. They unfolded as if in slow-motion. In their opening phases, attacks were marked by periods of intense shelling. Often these artillery barrages would not lead to anything more. They would just stop. Or, sometimes, there would be a pause, before another hail of artillery was released. The Serb military worked hard at making their bombardments appear random, so it was difficult to predict whether a particular bout of shelling was the prelude to a full offensive. Serb forces rarely sought to attain their final objective swiftly. With limited forces they would very cautiously and methodically build up their offensive. A few tanks and other armoured vehicles spearheaded their attack, systematically reducing enemy positions one by one. Only after they had been destroyed would the infantry move in and take the position.

After gaining new ground the Serbs would invariably pause. With so many UN troops and observers present, they had to be wary of a possible international armed response. A pause enabled them to gauge the world's reaction. Also, it tended to make the attack appear like a limited or isolated incident – a moment of pique that would not continue. This usually succeeded in taking the sting out of any intended tough response. And even when the UN drew a line in the sand, the Serbs were patient: they could always stop and wait for another, more propitious moment.[1]

The 'safe area' of Srebrenica proved an ideal target for this strategy. The area was difficult to defend. Although the terrain was extremely hilly and densely forested, the enclave itself was relatively small. Measuring only ten by fifteen kilometres, the enclave was a neatly contained target for Serb artillery. Neither the Bosnian Army, nor the Dutch battalion, possessed the necessary artillery to respond effectively. This vulnerability was made worse by the concentration of both the civilian population and the main elements of the protecting UN force in the two towns within the enclave: Potočari and Srebrenica itself. Both towns were located in valleys that could be overlooked from the surrounding hills. Potočari was in direct view of Serb artillery positions to the north and north-east. Parts of Srebrenica were somewhat better hidden, but not enough to afford much protection. The whole town was within easy range of Serb artillery from the east, south and north.

The understrength Dutch battalion had two main bases in the enclave. The battalion headquarters and logistics unit, together with Charlie Company, were located in an abandoned battery factory in Potočari. Bravo Company was based in an old textile mill in Srebrenica. Both compounds were clearly marked and clearly visible to anyone in the surrounding hills. In addition to the two bases, thirteen observation posts (OPs) guarded the fifty-kilometre perimeter. The job of the ninety-five soldiers in the OPs (an average of seven to each), was to observe and report on all military activity. Like all UN personnel in Bosnia, the OP soldiers spent much of their time acting as bookkeepers: counting and logging every explosion, firefight and troop movement.

As for the Dutch soldiers' other duties, this remained a matter of perpetual confusion. Officially, according to UN Security Council Resolution 819 of 16 April 1993, the town of Srebrenica and its surrounding area constituted a 'safe area', which meant that it 'should be free from any armed attack or any other hostile act'. The area was also a demilitarized zone subject to a ceasefire agreement between the Serbs and Muslims. As part of this agreement, Dutch troops were to supervise and assist in disarming the Muslim soldiers within the enclave. However, this issue was confused by paragraph 5 of UN Security Council Resolution 836 of 4 June 1993, which stated that UN troops had

> to deter attacks against the safe areas, to monitor the ceasefire, to promote the withdrawal of military or paramilitary units other than those of the Government of the Republic of Bosnia and Herzegovina and to occupy some key points on the ground, in addition to participating in the delivery of humanitarian relief to the population . . .

The UN Security Council thus authorized Bosnian troops to remain in the safe area. This clashed with the principle of demilitarization. A second confusion centred on the issue of the use of force by UN troops. Paragraph 5 suggested that their job was merely to deter, not to fight. Paragraph 9, however, suggested more. It authorized UNPROFOR (the United Nations Protection Force),

> in carrying out the mandate defined in paragraph 5 above, acting in self-defence, to take the necessary measures, including the use of force, in reply to bombardments against the safe areas by any of the parties or to armed incursion into them or in the event of any deliberate obstruction in and around those areas to the freedom of movement of UNPROFOR or of protected humanitarian convoys.

Beyond deterring attacks, UN troops could also defend themselves against attacks. But how restrictive was this defence intended to be? By mentioning bombardments, incursions and obstructions, the words 'self-defence' clearly need not simply mean 'only if you are fired upon directly, you may fire back'. That it was not meant to be that restrictive was further supported by paragraph 10, which authorized the use of air power 'in and around the safe areas'. Yet another opportunity for a wider use of force was offered by a reference to Resolution 770, which had called upon countries 'to take nationally or through regional agencies or arrangements all measures necessary' to deliver humanitarian assistance.

Yet a broad interpretation of the possible use of force posed practical problems. By early July 1995, there were just 429 Dutch soldiers left in the enclave. Only half of those were infantry, the rest support and medical troops. And, although they had some thirty 'YPR' armoured infantry fighting vehicles, an array of anti-tank missile systems and half a dozen 81mm mortars, they were very low on fuel and ammunition. Meanwhile, there were thousands of armed Muslims based in the safe area, the ceasefire was regularly violated by both sides and humanitarian aid and military supply convoys were habitually obstructed by the Serbs. Given the inconsistent mandate and limited strength, the Dutch felt they could, in effect, do little more than watch, count, log and report violations.

The Serb attack on the safe area of Srebrenica began in the early morning of Thursday 6 July 1995, at 03.15. In quick succession, six rockets, fired from a Multiple Launch Rocket System (MLRS) to the north of the enclave, hit Srebrenica. Some forty-five minutes later,

Dutch observation posts (OPs) in the south-eastern part of the enclave reported that fighting had erupted all around them. OPs Delta, Kilo, Sierra and Foxtrot noted a cacophony of fire from small arms, machine guns, mortars, artillery and tanks.

The OPs were exposed and vulnerable. Most were located on the tops of hills; each flew a huge, blue UN flag. These positions gave the Dutch UN soldiers a good view of the surrounding area and enabled them to perform their observer role effectively. Also, by remaining clearly visible to all warring parties, the OPs emphasized the UN's impartiality. At the same time it was hoped that visibility would prevent OPs from being shelled by mistake. But it also meant that any military role, even in self-defence, was problematic. Though heavily sandbagged and armed with a .50-calibre Browning heavy machine gun, short-range anti-tank weapons and, in a number of instances, TOW or Dragon anti-tank missiles and an 81mm mortar, OPs were far from being a soldier's dream of an ideal defensive position.

During the first day Serb shelling was concentrated in the area surrounding OP Foxtrot, which was located on the 836-metre-high Mount Javor, just outside the far south-east corner of the enclave. This hill was one of three that shielded the major entrance road to Srebrenica and controlled a road running just south of the enclave. Gaining unimpeded access to this road had long been believed to be a prime Serb objective. It was an important supply route, and a large bauxite mine along it was owned by Rasko Dukić, a wealthy Serb who was reputedly a close confidant of Radovan Karadžić and a financier of the Bosnian Serb nationalist SDS (Serbian Democratic Party). Taking control of the three hills, including OP Foxtrot, would give Dukić undisturbed access to his property. But it would also give the Serbs the option to march on Srebrenica itself.

The seven Dutch soldiers in OP Foxtrot were in an uncomfortable position, being exposed to Serb positions on the hills to the east. At around 13.00 artillery fire began drawing closer to OP Foxtrot. Two shells exploded close by. A little later, two Serb tanks aimed directly at the OP. The tower on top of the OP, which contained a TOW long-range anti-tank missile, was damaged.

The commander of the Dutch battalion in the safe area, Lieutenant-Colonel Ton Karremans, a lanky 46-year old with a virtual regulation-style Dutch army moustache, faced an acute dilemma. Should he order the OP crew to return fire in a legitimate act of self-defence – and risk being flattened by superior Serb firepower? Should he request air support and thus threaten to flatten the Serbs? Or, should he try to defuse the developing crisis through diplomacy? Karremans chose the third option. Clarification was requested from the Bosnian Serbs. But their reaction was not helpful. Typically, the Serbs ducked a meaningful response and demanded that the Dutch request be put in writing.

Concerned about the safety of his southern OPs, Karremans telephoned Dutch Brigade-General Cees Nicolai to discuss possible air support for his threatened OP. As the chief of staff at the UNPRO-FOR command in Sarajevo, Nicolai ran day-to-day operations in Bosnia. Nicolai said that UNPROFOR was hesitant. He told Karremans that Carl Bildt, the European Union negotiator, was at that moment in Belgrade discussing the possible recognition of Bosnia-Herzegovina by Serbian President Slobodan Milošević, which, if successful, would be a major diplomatic breakthrough. UNPROFOR did not want a military incident to endanger these delicate negotiations. Also, Nicolai reminded Karremans that the use of air power could easily lead to escalation. A month or so before, two air raids on ammunition depots near the Bosnian Serb capital of Pale had led to the taking of some 375 UN hostages all over Bosnia. UNPROFOR did not want to risk a repeat performance simply because a few OPs were under fire. Moreover, UNPROFOR Directive 2/95 of 29 May that year was still in force. It stated that 'the execution of the mandate [was] secondary to the security of UN personnel' and that force could only be used as 'a last resort'.[2] Clearly, the risks air support might cause the Dutch troops in the enclave were not yet outweighed by the possible advantages. Around this time, the fighting abated for the day. The weather worsened, and heavy rain caused visibility to deteriorate.

The following day, Friday 7 July, a thick fog prevented serious engagement. Small-arms fire was heard, but only twenty-seven shells detonated in the morning. In the evening, sixteen shells hit Srebrenica, some falling close to the Dutch base.

Lieutenant-Colonel Karremans at this stage still did not believe that the safe area was under serious threat. In his assessment of the situation on Friday evening, he stated that the Serb activities were 'attempts to provoke and intimidate ABiH [Bosnian Army] and Dutchbat [Dutch battalion]'. He did not expect 'the seizure of OPs and/or parts of the enclave'. The Bosnian Serb Army (BSA) would try 'to neutralize' the Bosnian Army 'in the long term', but 'due to a shortage of infantry', Karremans argued, 'the BSA will not be able to seize the enclave in the short term'.[3] His superiors in Sarajevo and Zagreb accepted this evaluation. The Dutch Ministry of Defence, monitoring the situation anxiously from The Hague, was reassured.

During the night, the Dutch recorded another 275 shells and mortar rounds exploding in the enclave. On Saturday morning, 8 July, it remained misty, with only sporadic firing. But at 12.30, OP Foxtrot again found itself under direct fire. Shells exploded close by. At 13.45, a Serb tank achieved a direct hit. Part of the right side of the OP's front protective wall collapsed. Two more shells hit the wall some minutes later. The commander of the OP, Sergeant Frans van Rossum, radioed battalion headquarters and requested permission to evacuate the OP. Permission was granted, provided Van Rossum judged the situation sufficiently stable for the seven men to drive away safely in their YPR. In fact, the intensity of the firefight between Muslims and Serbs had escalated to such a point that it was no longer safe. The men anxiously waited, with the YPR engine running, for the firing to let up for a sufficient interval. Just when they thought this interval had arrived and were preparing to evacuate, they noticed a Serb T-54 tank no more than 100 metres away, its barrel pointed at them. After a moment of great panic, the Dutch realized that the Serbs were summoning them to surrender. At approximately 14.30, the seven Dutch soldiers were disarmed and their OP plundered by a group of around ten Serb soldiers. After some haggling, the Serbs allowed the Dutch to go down the hill and return to Srebrenica in their YPR.

At the bottom of the hill, the Dutch soldiers encountered a Muslim soldier putting up a roadblock with three civilians. Their vehicle was forced to stop. Sergeant Van Rossum radioed his company commander, who asked if he could see any anti-tank weapons? 'Negative,' he responded. The commander ordered them to drive through the barricade. The sergeant told his men to close the hatches. As the vehicle began to move forward again, there was suddenly a dull crack.

Private Raviv van Renssen had been hit in the head. He sank on his knees and then slumped between his comrades sitting in the back of the vehicle. The YPR thundered down the road towards Srebrenica, frantically requesting medical assistance over the radio. Finally they were met by an armoured ambulance. The critically wounded soldier was transferred. But just before they reached the field dressing station in Potočari, Van Renssen died.

With OP Foxtrot in their possession the Serbs immediately moved to cut off the road behind OP Uniform. A three-hour firefight ensued between Muslim forces, who were behind the Dutch, and Serbs, who were both in front of them and on their left flank. Sergeant Alwin van Eck and his men noticed five Muslim soldiers with anti-tank weapons on the road behind them. Mindful of what happened to the men of OP Foxtrot, they dared not abandon their post. By 18.30, Serb infantry had completed their occupation of the ridge behind the Dutch. Shortly afterwards, twenty to thirty Serb soldiers moved in to take over the OP. After robbing the Dutch of their equipment, the Serbs told the tense UN soldiers that they could either leave for Srebrenica or become their prisoners. The OP squad judged the latter choice to be the safer. The remaining observation posts heard Van Eck over their radios: 'OP Uniform here, we can leave. The Serbs vouch for our safety. But we have to hurry. The men are becoming nervous, they want to drive on.'[4]

OP Sierra, further west down the Jadar river valley, had a quieter day. Most of the shooting had taken place over their heads. None the less, they too were in danger of being cut off. They considered pre-empting the Serbs by abandoning their position, but they were worried about the Muslim forces behind them. That evening – compliments of the Serbs – they got a message from their captured comrades: 'OP Sierra had better stay where they are, it is too dangerous to move because all ABiH [Bosnian Army] has not left the area.'[5] They also received a message that the men from OP Uniform were on their way to a hotel for the night and that the Serbs would allow them to leave for Holland soon after.

Despite the loss of two of his observation posts, Lieutenant-Colonel Karremans still did not think that the Serbs were after the whole safe area. He saw no reason to change his assessment of twenty-four hours before:

The attacks on OP Foxtrot and OP Uniform must be regarded
as part of an attempt to take possession of the Jadar valley. The
fact that there are no attacks on the rest of the enclave perimeter
reinforces this view.

Karremans regarded the shelling on Srebrenica as 'a diversion and an
attempt at intimidation'.[6] There was, however, one change in plans.
Karremans had always assumed that, in case of trouble, the OPs would
fall back on the Dutch bases in the towns of Srebrenica or Potočari.
But this option had become too risky. It was now left to the individual
commanders of each OP to decide whether to withdraw or surrender
to the Serbs. They were informed that the safety of their personnel
was paramount.

Karremans also offered to release the weapons the UN peacekeepers
had collected from the Bosnians over the past two years. The arms
were stored in a 'weapons collection point' in Srebrenica. The acting
commander of the Bosnian Army in Srebrenica, Ramiz Bečirević,
had asked Karremans to release the weapons two days earlier, but at
that point Karremans had refused because the Serbs had not crossed
the safe-area perimeter. This time, Bečirević showed no interest in
regaining the two tanks and sundry small arms. Not only did he have
no ammunition for these weapons, Bečirević also feared that accepting
them would both give the Serbs a cause to attack the enclave further
and absolve the Dutch from helping the Muslims. So he told Karremans: 'We don't want to take the weapons. Why don't you call for
air strikes?'

To observe the movements of the Serbs and make up for the loss
of the southern OPs, the commander of Bravo Company, Captain
Jelte Groen, decided to deploy his Quick Reaction Force of four
armoured vehicles around the town of Srebrenica. They were told to
take up two separate positions a few kilometres south of the town.
But one of the armoured vehicles ran into Bosnian forces, who threatened the Dutch crew. The Muslims demanded that the Dutch move
further south towards the Serbs and attempted to block the YPR's
withdrawal route by moving a car wreck on to the road behind them.
When the Dutch tried to prevent this a hand grenade was thrown at
them. They suffered no damage but returned quickly to Srebrenica
to take up an alternative position west of the town.

By Saturday night the main Bosnian Army strategy of defending the enclave was failing. Outgunned by the Serbs, their best chance of turning the tables on their enemy was to get UN forces engaged. The most likely way of achieving this was to manoeuvre the Dutch into the Serb line of fire so that at some point they had no option but to fire back in self-defence and to call in air support. The Muslims could not allow the Dutch to fall back to their compounds. But the attempts to prevent this had backfired. The killing of Raviv van Renssen had made the Dutch so wary of the Muslims that they seemed more prepared to surrender to the Serbs than to withdraw. The Serbs exploited this development to the full. They made sure that all of the remaining OPs were aware of how well the Dutch prisoners were being treated.

The question of whether the Serb objective was to secure the southern road and the Jadar river valley or to take over the whole enclave was settled on Sunday 9 July. OP Sierra fell to the Serbs at 09.00 that morning. None the less, Karremans still believed the Serbs had limited objectives. He reported to UNPROFOR that he expected to lose the remaining OPs on the southern border of the enclave (Delta and Kilo) located some kilometres west of the OPs already lost. Indeed, OP Kilo was overrun at 18.15 on Sunday evening. Meanwhile Sergeant Ruud Zuurman, the OP Delta commander, decided to move his men out rather than surrender to the Serbs. But they were stopped en route to Srebrenica by Muslim soldiers in the village of Kutuzero and held overnight.

Should Karremans request air support? This was the question Karremans constantly asked himself. The Dutch believed they could not be expected to put up any meaningful defence of the enclave. They were convinced that air power was the only weapon available to compensate for the weakness on the ground. Still, Karremans was aware of the problems posed by the use of air power. In his report to UNPROFOR that Sunday he concluded:

> Using CAS [Close Air Support] in all possible ways is in my opinion not feasible yet. It will provoke the BSA in such way that both Srebrenica itself and OPs and compounds will be targeted by all means. Especially the MLRS M-63 north of OP(NL)P, the MLRS M-77 within Bratunac and all their

artillery and mortars will launch their missiles and rounds at fixed targets. Unless these weaponsystems could be eliminated in once [*sic*] which is hardly impossible [read: 'possible'].

Although Karremans had discussed air support as soon as the Serbs had started shelling OP Foxtrot on Thursday, his reservations about the use of air power grew. Although the indications that the Serbs wanted the whole enclave multiplied (Karremans knew, by this time, from information radioed through by the captured Dutch soldiers, that there was a considerable concentration of Serb firepower to the east of the enclave), Karremans remained convinced that this was not an immediate aim. At the same time, he became increasingly conscious of the vulnerability of his soldiers to potential Serb retaliation and less willing to risk their lives. For air support to be effective, the artillery and mortar threat to Srebrenica and Potočari had to be taken out at the same time as the forces attacking the OPs. This would mean a massive operation and a serious escalation in the stakes. Karremans, as well as his superiors in Sarajevo and Zagreb, were in a quandary.

In The Hague, Defence Minister Voorhoeve was also very worried. He told the US ambassador, Terry Dornbush, that although he was not sure the Serbs were going to overrun the enclave, he was 'very pessimistic' and described the situation as 'hopeless'. The Dutch were 'outnumbered' and 'surrounded'; the city was 'indefensible'. Uncorroborated evidence states that he said that he was 'wary of air strikes' because these could lead to greater civilian casualties. The evidence also indicates that on the same day, a call by the United States in NATO in Brussels for air strikes was countered by the Dutch ambassador to NATO as 'dangerous' and 'counterproductive'.

In the southern part of the enclave, the situation had continued to deteriorate. Hundreds of Muslim refugees had begun to stream north from the so-called Swedish Shelter Project in the Jadar valley. An armoured vehicle sent south by Captain Groen to check things out and take up a new observation post was surprised and captured by the Serbs. By noon on Sunday 9 July, the hamlet of Pusmulići, three kilometres south of Srebrenica, was in flames. The Serbs moved north along the main road to Srebrenica and also tracked over the hills to the west. By around 18.30 on Sunday, when the fighting died down, they were within two kilometres of the town.

That evening Dutchbat busily consulted the higher UN commands on what to do the next day. The assessment that they were dealing with a limited attack had proved wrong. How could the Serbs be stopped? The highest UN commander in the former Yugoslavia, French Lieutenant-General Bernard Janvier, was concerned that air support would lead to immediate escalation with the Serbs. On the advice of Dutch Colonel Harm de Jonge, the staff officer responsible for operations, Janvier decided that Dutchbat should make a stand. At around 22.00, the battalion received the following order:

> you must take up blocking positions using all means available in order to prevent further penetration and advance of BSA units in the direction of Srebrenica. Every possible measure must be taken to reinforce these positions, including measures relating to weapons.[7]

This meant that the Dutch had to move some of their white-painted YPRs into positions around Srebrenica that were clearly visible to the advancing Serbs. The action was intended to convey the message 'up to here and no further'. If the Serbs persisted, the Dutch would open fire.

When the order arrived by fax to Bravo Company in Srebrenica, Sergeant Arthur Batalona, who was manning the operations room, later recalled,

> Everybody got a fright. You could easily get killed in such an operation. As far as I knew, we had not been sent to Srebrenica to defend the enclave, but rather as some kind of spruced-up observers.[8]

More senior commanders were worried as well. Not only was Dutchbat not well equipped for such a task, but, as an airmobile unit, its men also lacked the training for combat with armoured vehicles.

Still, Bravo Company tried to make the best of it. They managed to muster fifty men in six YPRs with .50-calibre machine guns, two medium-range Dragon anti-tank missile systems and some short-range AT4 anti-tank weapons. An 81mm mortar was readied within the compound in Srebrenica for fire support. The men received their instructions at 03.30 on Sunday morning. An hour and a half later, positions Bravo One and Bravo Four, respectively west and south of the town, were occupied by two YPRs each. Two more YPRs were moving to positions Bravo Two, further to the south, and Bravo Three, on the east.

To back up the blocking positions, General Janvier and Yasushi Akashi, the UN Secretary-General's Special Representative in the former Yugoslavia, sent an ultimatum to the Serbs. From Zagreb, they demanded that the Serbs halt their attack and withdraw to the enclave's border. The Serbs must also release the captured Dutch soldiers with all of their equipment. The Serbs were notified that Dutch troops had taken up blocking positions south of Srebrenica and if they were attacked by BSA forces, 'NATO Close Air Support will be employed'.

Akashi and Janvier were very wary of escalating the conflict. For that reason, they agreed – and let the Serbs know this as well – that the air attacks for the next day would only take the form of close air support, that is, only those Serb forces that were seen to be firing at Dutch positions would be attacked. At 22.30, General Nicolai conveyed the ultimatum to the Serbs in a telephone call from Sarajevo. He talked to Mladić's deputy, General Zdravko Tolimir, who did not even let him finish: 'What are you talking about? There are no Serbs in the enclave. General, you should not blindly trust Muslim propaganda.'[9]

Captain Groen, the Bravo Company commander, was aware of the restrictions put on the use of force. He knew that, as he wrote later,

> we were here for one thing only and that is the security of the civilians . . . If we openly took sides with the ABiH [Bosnian Army] soldiers by opening fire (with them) on the Serbs, other than in self-defence, we would possibly lose our UN status in the eyes of the BSA and would be considered their enemy together with the ABiH. If this were to happen all protection for the civilians would be lost and, of course, so would all protection for the UN personnel in the enclave.[10]

In order to avoid immediate escalation, Groen instructed his troops not to aim their fire directly at the enemy. Only if they were directly attacked, should they aim at the Serbs.

★

The wait for daybreak of Monday 10 July was an uneasy one for the Dutch soldiers in the blocking positions. Some were certain they would die. In the morning Serb guns opened up again on Srebrenica. The number of shells hitting the town appeared to be increasing. Sergeant Frank Struik had been taping the fighting around OP Hotel (from which he could observe the whole south-eastern corner of the enclave) since the previous day with his Walkman:

> Damn, they are firing at us, those idiots. Bastards . . . There's one coming. Boom. Mortars. Another one. Bang. Whine . . . whack, here it comes. One, two, ah, these are correct bingos.[11]

The deputy Bravo Company commander, Captain Peter Hageman, who was in charge of the blocking positions, was supposed to occupy Bravo Two, the most advanced position. But he and his men never reached the intended location. The track proved impassable for their YPR. When he tried to move towards an alternative position, a Serb tank opened fire. Suddenly, a shell exploded close by and the YPR went off the road. The vehicle was undamaged, but stuck. The crew failed to get it back on the road. They joined Bravo Four on the outskirts of Srebrenica on foot. By nine in the morning, the Dutch battalion headquarters requested air support, but they were told to update their list of targets first, since the most recent list was some twenty hours old. The Serbs had advanced since then. But, slowly, the fighting around the town died down and air support no longer seemed urgent. The NATO aircraft that had been in the air on stand-by returned to base in Italy at 14.00 because of deteriorating weather. US sources maintain that Defence Minister Voorhoeve told the Americans in The Hague that he believed that the situation was 'stabilizing' and that he would only favour close air support if the Serbs resumed their attack. He opposed 'retaliation for retaliation's sake'.

The heaviest fighting that morning was concentrated less than two kilometres south of Srebrenica, in the area of Pusmulići. The Serbs were consolidating their grip on the south-eastern corner of the enclave in preparation for the attack on Srebrenica. They had carefully avoided the blocking positions and thus the danger of air attacks.

More and more refugees from the southern parts of the enclave began to congregate in Srebrenica's market square. During the afternoon, the Bosnian defences south of the town collapsed. Around eighty Bosnian soldiers passed Bravo Four at around six. Among them, a Dutch soldier recognized the Muslim hairdresser who used to cut his hair in Potočari. The Bosnian soldiers told the dozen or so Dutch that they would be taking up new positions in the town to continue the fight. The number of refugees streaming past continued to increase. After the afternoon's hiatus, it became clear, just after 18.00, that the Serbs were about to resume their advance on Srebrenica.

OP Hotel noticed some eighty Serb soldiers lining up above Srebrenica, on the hairpin bend in the road, ready to descend on the town. They were taking their time, making sure the Muslim civilians in the town saw them as well. The civilians began to panic and started fleeing northwards. Finally, at 18.30, the Serbs began to advance. Bravo One was ordered by their company commander to open fire. As a warning, they aimed over the Serbs' heads, while the 81mm mortar only fired flares. The exposed Dutch peacekeepers were terrified. Pandemonium broke out among the Muslim civilians. Hundreds streamed toward the Dutch compound. The fear-stricken mob broke through the gates, frantically seeking shelter and protection with the Dutch soldiers.

Captain Hageman was afraid that his positions were being circumvented. He concentrated his YPRs near the market square. Bravo Four was also firing in the direction of the Serbs. However, the Serbs continued to gain ground, necessitating yet another redeployment of Hageman's YPRs, this time further into the town, near the school. Captain Hageman's stated goal was to be able to aim more directly at the Serbs: falling back would allow him to do this.

Yet the Bosnian troops would not allow it. They did not believe Hageman intended to put up serious resistance and feared the Dutch just wanted to get away from the fight. They threatened him with anti-tank weapons if he tried to move. An appeal to the mayor of the town of Srebrenica, Fahrudin Salihović, was ineffective. He did not trust Dutch intentions either.

The Serbs continued to push forward, but cautiously. Like the Dutch, they were anxiously watching the skies. Would the UN finally decide on air attacks? At around 19.30, the Serbs were seen withdrawing in a westerly direction. By 20.00 the fighting had died down. The Serbs seemed to want to give the refugees time to get out of Srebrenica and flee to Potočari, before taking the town.

The Dutch, unintentionally, almost hastened this process by moving to evacuate the people from Srebrenica to the main Dutch base in Potočari. But the evacuation plan met with resistance from the Bosnian

Army. They knew that their only chance of holding on to the enclave was to get the United Nations involved in the fighting. To this end, they needed to keep the Dutch troops in the front line, but it would help if the civilian population were caught up in the fighting as well. People who had already left for Potočari were being turned back by Muslim soldiers. Mayor Salihović supported this line of action, so the refugees stayed in Srebrenica during the night of 10 and 11 July.

There could no longer be any doubt that the Serb objective was the capture of the whole enclave. Although General Ratko Mladić, the commander of the Bosnian Serb Army, had denied this to General Janvier the previous day and repeated the pledge not to conquer the enclave as late as the evening of 10 July, this was clearly a blatant lie. The UN ultimatum of the previous evening had had no effect whatsoever. The attack had not been halted and none of the captured Dutch soldiers had been released. What should the UN do now?

As Karremans had fallen ill, his deputy, Major Rob Franken, requested air support in his stead at 19.00, when the Serb attack was in full swing. Franken, aware of the problem of Serb retaliation, submitted three sets of targets. The priority target area was the Serb forces south of the blocking positions. But almost as important were Serb artillery positions north of the enclave and on the high plateau south-east of Srebrenica, near Pribićevac. If left intact, these could wreak havoc on both UN and civilian targets in Potočari and Srebrenica. In total, Franken wanted around forty targets destroyed.

Getting the go-ahead for air support was a time-consuming process that usually took at least two hours. In accordance with instruction UNPROFOR OPO 14/94, Dutchbat first had to lodge the request with Sector North East in Tuzla. At the time of the crisis, Dutchbat was fortunate to be dealing with a Dutch colonel, Charlef Brantz, who, as the acting sector commander, was sympathetic to their situation and passed on the requests as quickly as possible to the next rung on the ladder, UNPROFOR in Sarajevo. At UNPROFOR, the request had to be approved by Lieutenant-General Rupert Smith, the British commander. During the assault on Srebrenica, Smith was away. His French deputy, Major-General Hervé Gobilliard, and particularly, since they were dealing with a Dutch battalion, chief of staff General Nicolai, had assumed responsibility. If they approved, the request would be passed on to the UN Protection Force's highest headquarters (known as UNPF from spring 1995) in the former Yugoslavia, in Zagreb. There, General Janvier would first consider the matter with his military aides. He would then consult the UN Secretary-General's Special Representative, Yasushi Akashi. If they agreed, the request would be passed on to NATO.

NATO was normally put on alert some time before the actual approval of the use of air power. But they would not know the full details of what type of targets were approved until Akashi and Janvier had decided. The NATO Air Operations Coordination Centre (AOCC) in Vicenza in Italy strived always to have some aircraft from the 5th Allied Tactical Air Force in the air. Since 9 July, AOCC had had two F-16s airborne on continuous alert during daytime for close air support. Still, an actual attack by only two aircraft would involve a major operation. Since the shooting down of American pilot Scott O'Grady over Bosnia in June, NATO had become very concerned about the Serbian anti-aircraft threat. In response, aircraft on standby now were either on ground alert or circled in a holding area above the Adriatic, rather than over Bosnia, thus adding to their flight time to targets. No plane was allowed into Bosnian airspace without the protection of a whole string of other aircraft: especially those designed to suppress enemy missile air defences (SEAD) and others to destroy air defence radars with so-called HARM missiles. The numbers of such SEAD-aircraft was limited. Also, even with air-refuelling, no aircraft could stay in the air indefinitely. An attack at night or in bad weather was even more difficult, since only the US Air Force had aircraft capable of performing such missions in theatre.

The chain of events leading to the UN's inaction that Monday night was complex. Following the 19.00 request from Franken, which was approved and passed on by Tuzla and Sarajevo, General Janvier convened a meeting of the Crisis Action Team fifty minutes later. Present were his top advisers: his two French military assistants, the Dutch chief of staff Major-General Ton Kolsteren, Colonel Harm de Jonge and the staff officers responsible for intelligence, air operations and NATO liaison, as well as Akashi's assistant, John Almstrom. The broad consensus among the officers was to give air support. De Jonge told Janvier: 'You gave Mladić a strong warning yesterday and he is defying you. We must give air support.'[12] The British air operations officer noted the risks that the captured Dutch soldiers ran if air attacks occurred, but agreed 'we must act'. Even Almstrom came out in support: 'If the forces are under fire, we have no choice. Akashi will be back at half past eleven, but for a "Blue Sword" operation we do not have to wait for him.'[13]

Only Janvier hesitated. He faced a momentous decision. Even if he only agreed to a 'Blue Sword' operation, that is, a close air support mission in Bosnia, Janvier feared that it might not be enough and would need to be followed up by larger-scale air strikes against more than a handful of Serb targets. This would risk drawing UNPRO-FOR into an all-out war with the Serbs. Janvier wanted more information and further consultation. He ordered NATO aircraft to be put on alert, but also wanted to know when NATO would be ready to attack. The American NATO liaison officer left the room to check the matter with AOCC. Janvier asked how the Dutch government felt about air support. General Kolsteren left the meeting to phone Voorhoeve in The Hague. Janvier himself got in touch with Sarajevo to get the view from acting UNPROFOR commander General Gobilliard. Gobilliard was not available. At about 21.05, Janvier got hold of Akashi. Immediately thereafter he phoned Mladić and spoke to either him or his deputy, General Tolimir. Kolsteren reported at 21.10 that Voorhoeve did not object to air support. NATO aircraft were by then airborne above the Adriatic: they could hit their targets within half an hour of the order to go in.

Janvier still hesitated. He could not quite understand why Mladić would want to take, or even punish, the enclave while EU negotiator Carl Bildt was engaged in talks with President Milošević in Belgrade. By this time it was getting dark. The Serbs' attack on Srebrenica had stopped. Close air support was no longer necessary. Darkness also made it difficult to tell the Dutch, Muslim and Serb units apart from the air. But what should happen if, at dawn, the Serbs resumed their attack? Janvier decided around 22.00: 'Tomorrow at six, NATO has to be ready. If necessary, I will approve air support, but not if the threat only comes from infantry.'[14] The ultimatum of the previous night was to be repeated to the Serbs. The only difference was that this time they were not told about the nature of the air attacks.

In the Netherlands, Defence Minister Voorhoeve was forty minutes late in arriving at the studio for his appearance on a late-night current-affairs programme on television. On it he announced that 'you cannot let the enclave just be run over'. It was his view that 'the blackest scenario now has become reality. Air actions are now inevitable.' Though taking a tough line in public Voorhoeve was privately extremely concerned for the safety of the Dutch troops. In the morning, Voorhoeve and his advisers decided that Dutchbat was in a 'no-win situation with great risks', according to the chief of defence staff, General Henk van den Breemen. 'Under these circumstances', they argued, 'the security of our people must be paramount.'[15] General Van den Breemen was dispatched to Zagreb to meet Janvier 'face to face'.

Within the enclave, it was a night of feverish activity. At around 21.00, one of the OP commanders held by the Serbs in Bratunac radioed in to the battalion. The Serbs had asked him to convey an ultimatum. Dutchbat was given forty-eight hours to evacuate the enclave, starting from 06.00 the next morning. The Serbs guaranteed a safe evacuation for the battalion and the Muslim population. But by midnight, the anxious Dutch troops were informed by their commanding officers that the UN had given an ultimatum to the Serbs: 'The BSA must withdraw starting from 06.00 hrs; failure to do so will result in large-scale air strikes.'[16]

Here were the beginnings of a tragic misunderstanding between UNPF and Dutchbat about the scale and conditions of the air support. Janvier and Akashi had decided no such ultimatum. They had only agreed that *if* the Dutch were attacked, actively attacking Serb forces, or 'smoking guns', could be bombed from the air. This misunderstanding was compounded by another. The Dutchbat commanders, as well as Sector North East, believed that, no matter what, there would be massive air strikes against all of the forty targets they had identified the previous day and anything new that moved.

Lieutenant-Colonel Karremans met with the Bosnian Army command and the civilian town council in the Srebrenica post office shortly after midnight. To a sceptical audience, he announced 'Gentlemen, I have an important message.' The room fell silent. 'The Serbs have received an ultimatum. They have to withdraw before 06 00. Otherwise there will be bombing everywhere.' On a map, Karremans pointed out a number of places in and around the enclave that would be attacked from the air the next morning at six. The road into the enclave along which the Serbs were attacking would become 'a death zone'. Forty to sixty aircraft would be employed to bomb the Serbs.

The Muslims no longer believed him. Mayor Fahrudin Salihović twice asked if Karremans could guarantee that the attack would take place? Karremans twice answered: 'Don't shoot the piano-player.' The interpreter, Hasan Nuhanović, did not quite understand the expression, which he translated as 'don't trouble the bringer of good tidings'. Karremans also informed them that the Dutch would again take up the blocking positions they had held on Monday. He wanted the Muslims to protect his flanks. Karremans left the meeting at two in the morning, believing that the Bosnian Army would do this.

Yet, during the night there were many signs that the Bosnian defence had collapsed. OP Hotel had witnessed withdrawals early in the evening. In Srebrenica, Dutch soldiers noted that around 300 Bosnian Army men had disappeared in a westerly direction. Despite the earlier resistance of the Bosnian command, large groups of refugees, with armed men among them, were moving north in the direction of Potočari. In the north-west, where OP Mike was located (and from where, later, the majority of Muslim men would try to escape), Dutch soldiers saw fighting breaking out among Bosnian soldiers.

The Dutch prepared for daybreak. Around 04.00, a call to Sector North East in Tuzla confirmed that an air attack was planned for just before 07.00. The list with the forty 'hard targets' from the previous day was discussed. Around 06.00 blocking positions Bravo One and Bravo Three were again occupied. Forward Air Controllers were ready to guide the aircraft to their targets. It was a clear morning.

The first NATO aircraft took off from air bases in Italy at 06.00. Their 'time over target' was set at 06.50. A massive fleet of some sixty AWACS early warning and command aircraft, air defence fighters, anti-air defence and electronic jamming aircraft, tankers and others was in the air to support less than a dozen aircraft designated to attack the ground targets around Srebrenica. The Dutch were waiting for the attack to begin automatically at the earliest opportunity. Meanwhile UNPF and UNPROFOR were waiting to be contacted by Dutchbat when the Serbs attacked again. As was appropriate with a 'Blue Sword' close air support mission, only actively attacking forces could be designated as targets.

At 08.00, Dutchbat queried the lack of air support. But Sector North East was unable to pass on the query quickly. The person responsible for air support was not present and the secure fax machine was not working properly owing to a recent spell of bad weather. The message got stuck.

Around 09.30, the commander of the blocking positions went on a reconnaissance mission. He drove past the point where Bravo Four had been stationed the previous day and then on to the hairpin bend west of Srebrenica. While moving up the hill, he spotted a tank and a number of trucks near the transmitter tower further up the road.

At 10.00, Dutchbat again requested air support. This time, they sent a fresh list of targets. Forty minutes later, Sector North East managed to fax the list to Sarajevo. Sarajevo passed it on to Janvier and Akashi before 11.00. To make sure something happened, Colonel Brantz in Tuzla phoned The Hague and implored Defence Minister Voorhoeve to get in touch with the highest UN authorities. Voorhoeve phoned Akashi to convince him of the urgency of the situation.

Shortly after 11.00, the Serb attack on Srebrenica resumed. The situation deteriorated quickly. Captain Groen obtained permission from battalion HQ to let his men fire at will. The Serbs were now, for once, moving forward fast, along the high ridge to the west of Srebrenica. Meanwhile, they were pounding the town from the east. A tank opened fire on Bravo One. A small team of Dutch commandos and three British SAS troops were accompanying Bravo One in a Mercedes jeep. They formed a Tactical Air Control Party, whose job was to guide NATO aircraft to their targets. But the Serbs understood that the Dutch were deploying their Forward Air Controllers and fired warning shots at the blocking position, slightly injuring one Dutch commando.

'The situation was untenable,' according to Corporal Hans Berkers in Bravo One, 'it turned out that they'd zeroed in on us. They had already been firing at the Muslims in the same spot. Fifteen metres away shells were exploding. They were firing high explosive. Then we withdrew. For this we could not risk our lives.'[17] Bravo One redeployed. The commandos took off their highly visible blue helmets and went their own way in search of a better position from which to guide the expected NATO aircraft to their targets.

Bosnian soldiers deserted their positions around Srebrenica. Captain

Groen decided to abandon the positions of Bravo Three and Bravo Four again and withdraw his men, as on the previous day, to the market square. He did not expect the remaining Bosnians to hold out for more than half an hour.

By this point the Dutch were ready to give up. Battalion HQ ordered all troops to withdraw to the compound in Srebrenica. Groen ordered Bravo One to get back into town. Shells were now landing close to the Dutch compound in Srebrenica as well. Four to five thousand desperate refugees were grouped in and around the compound. The most frightening moment, according to private Jord Honig, came

> when a Serb mortar shell hit close to the entrance of the compound. The spot was full of civilians who had fled to our UN-post in a panic. A UN vehicle – by chance unmanned – was completely destroyed. I do not know how many dead there were. It was a terrible sight. Most of us had never seen anything like it. While we were trying like mad to get the wounded to safety, we expected the next mortar attack. We should have been in the bunker. As a soldier you know: the first shell is only to zero in, then you get direct hits.[18]

Two more shells hit a little further away. Still, Honig believed that the Serbs 'were not aiming at the blue helmets, they were more clever than that. But we did not dare to be too sure.'

The Dutch resumed the evacuation of refugees to Potočari that had been stymied the day before by Bosnian soldiers. When the refugees saw that the soldiers were getting their trucks ready to get the wounded out first, they stormed the vehicles and would not be moved. At 14.30, the first trucks left, with refugees on the roofs and bumpers and hanging from the mirrors.

Ironically, minutes later the first air raid started. The second request for air support that day had finally been granted shortly after noon. The authorization was still limited to close air support. The order, signed by Janvier, read:

> I recommend that UN release authority for *Blue Sword* be issued for attacks on any forces attacking the blocking UNPROFOR position south of Srebrenica and heavy weapons identified as shelling UN positions in Srebrenica town.

Unfortunately, the aircraft that had been airborne since 06.00 that morning had returned to base by 11.30. The Serbs, who had not moved while the aircraft were circling the skies, had cleverly resumed the attack on Srebrenica after air defence radars in Serbia noticed the NATO aircraft were returning to base.

It took time to put together a new 'package' of eighteen aircraft. 'Time over target' was only expected to be 13.45. The first two aircraft had some difficulties establishing contact with the Dutch commandos who performed the Forward Air Controller role. The two Dutch F-16s reached the target area at around 14.30. One of the commandos, just west of Srebrenica, guided the female pilot to targets near the transmitter tower. After a dry run, despite noticing some anti-aircraft fire, she went in for the attack. The commando called out:

'Here Windmill zero-two, everything south of the track you just flew is hostile. Blow them away!'

'Windmill zero-two, between that house with the red roof and that barn I see tanks driving on the road. Confirm?'

'Roger Alpha, get that shit.'

'Roger, coming in.'[19]

The pilot then released a Mk 82 gravity bomb 'off hot', that is, armed. The second pilot came in from the north. In the attacks, one Serb tank was destroyed and another damaged. The pilots received no confirmation from the ground of their success: the Tactical Air Control party was under heavy Serb fire.

After a quarter of an hour, the next pair of F-16s, this time American, arrived over eastern Bosnia. They had been assigned a Serb artillery piece firing from a position north-west of the enclave. Because the terrain was heavily forested and had no major distinctive geographical features, the commando air controllers on the ground lit green smoke flares to guide the aircraft to their targets. But the Americans failed to see the smoke and returned to base.

The waiting was now for the slow-flying A-10 heavy ground-attack aircraft that were to attack an artillery position that was firing on Potočari from the north. But the Serb response preempted them. The Serbs sent a swift ultimatum: if the air attacks were not stopped forthwith, they would kill the captured Dutch soldiers and shell the refugees and Dutchbat indiscriminately. One of the captured OP commanders telephoned OP Papa from Bratunac with this message. As soon as Colonel Brantz in Tuzla heard the news, he phoned Sarajevo and The Hague.

The response from The Hague was swift. When Brantz phoned, both the Prime Minister, Wim Kok, and the Foreign Minister, Hans van Mierlo, were present in the 'bunker'. Bypassing regular UN and NATO channels, Voorhoeve got directly in touch with the Air Operations Coordination Centre in Vicenza. The Dutch liaison officer there, a rather surprised Colonel Arjen Koopmans, picked up the phone and heard a loud 'Stop, stop, stop!' emanating from the receiver.[20] Fortunately for the minister, Akashi and UNPROFOR in Sarajevo had also arrived at the same conclusion. The air raids were officially called off.

Meanwhile, the evacuation of Srebrenica continued apace. The Serbs continued to shell the surroundings so as to speed up the process. Private Honig saw

> an old woman crawling on her hands and knees, bleeding. Children had lost their parents. Everywhere was luggage, dumped to run faster. There were people sitting at the side of the road, exhausted. We tried to get them up: 'To Potočari, Četniks come!' we shouted . . . We covered half the route running, my mates and I, looking for cover from yard to yard. After that we got a lift from a YPR. That wasn't really allowed. Our physical presence on the road to Potočari was meant to protect the people. But the sergeant pulled us in: 'First you lot in safety.'[21]

When the last people had left the town, Captain Groen ordered his troops in the blocking position to fall back and cover the retreat. The commandos of the Tactical Air Control Party came running back to the compound, just in time to be picked up by the departing Bravo Company. A little after 16.00, on 11 July, the town of Srebrenica fell to the Serbs.

The fall of the whole enclave was imminent. Although the Dutch tried to form a cordon between the refugees and the advancing Serb forces, they could not stem the Serbian tide, and all of the refugees were forced towards the Dutch compound in Potočari. In the early evening, Karremans opened ceasefire negotiations with the Serbs. The next stage in the tragedy of the fall of Srebrenica was about to begin.

NOTES

1. See James Gow, *Triumph of the Lack of Will: International Diplomacy and the Yugoslav War* (London: Hurst, 1996), and James Gow, 'Coercive Cadences: The Yugoslav War of Dissolution', in Lawrence Freedman, ed., *Strategic Coercion* (forthcoming).

2. Brigade-General O. van der Wind, *Rapport gebaseerd op de Debriefing Srebrenica* ('*Report Based on the Srebrenica Debriefing*') (Assen, 4 October 1995), p. 16 (henceforth cited as *Debriefing*).

3. *Debriefing*, p. 25.

4. Bas Mesters, 'Tussen twee vuren in Srebrenica' ('In the firing line in Srebrenica'), *De Volkskrant*, 29 July 1995.

5. *Debriefing*, p. 27.

6. *Debriefing*, p. 27.

7. *Debriefing*, p. 30.

8. 'Een cynisch spelletje Stratego' ('A cynical game of "Stratego"'), *Algemeen Dagblad*, 14 October 1995.

9. Frank Westerman, 'VN voorkwamen aanval op Srebrenica' ('UN prevented attack on Srebrenica'), *NRC/Handelsblad*, 14 October 1995.

10. *Dutchbat in Vredesnaam, Januari 1995–Juli 1995* (*Dutchbat in the Name of Peace, January 1995–July 1995*) (Rijswijk: Début, 1996), p. 296.

11. *De Volkskrant*, 29 July 1996.

12. Frank Westerman, 'We need F-16's swooping down now', *NRC/Handelsblad*, 29 May 1996.

13. *NRC/Handelsblad*, 29 May 1996.

14. *NRC/Handelsblad*, 29 May 1996.

15. Henk van den Breemen, 'Hollands Dagboek' ('Dutch Diary'), *NRC/Handelsblad*, 22 July 1995.

16. *Debriefing*, p. 34.

17. Ward op den Brouw and Harry Meijer, 'Serviërs zijn voor de Dutchbatters nu de "good guys"' ('Serbs are now the "good guys" to the Dutchbat soldiers'), *NRC/Handelsblad*, 24 July 1995.

18. Wilma Kieskamp, 'We konden niet al die vluchtelingen op onze rug nemen' ('We couldn't carry all those refugees on our backs'), *Trouw*, 29 July 1995.

19. Leo de Rooij, 'F16's: Succes met een nasmaak' ('F16's: Success with an aftertaste'), *Defensiekrant*, 27 July 1995.

20. Frank Westerman, 'Spookrijders in Srebrenica' ('Ghost-drivers in Srebrenica'), *NRC/Handelsblad*, 11 November 1995.

21. *Trouw*, 29 July 1995.

CHAPTER TWO

The Deportation

By the evening of 11 July there were around 25,000 Muslim refugees packed together in and around the Dutch compound in Potočari. The vast majority of the refugees were women and children, but there were also an estimated 1,200 men of military age, as well as many more who were either too young or too old for military service.

The Dutch had let, perhaps, between 3,000 and 4,000 refugees into the compound through a hole they cut in the fence. But when the factory hall in which the refugees were accommodated was judged to be full, the fence was closed off. Around 20,000 people found themselves stuck outside the compound. They sought shelter in empty factory halls in the surrounding area.

With thousands of refugees continuing to stream into Potočari, the Dutch soldiers saw a humanitarian nightmare unfolding before them. Lieutenant Eelco Koster later described the scene:

> It was absolute chaos. Women were walking around crying, searching for their children, family or friends. Children were calling for their mother ... Women, men and children with gunshot and other wounds ... were asking for a doctor ... People were fainting. A couple of pregnant women spontaneously went into labour because of the tension. Medics worked overtime with the little material they could still use.[1]

Though the Dutch shared their water and food with refugees, supplies were totally inadequate. Some women grew so desperate that they risked encounters with Serb soldiers by scouring abandoned houses in Potočari in search of food and water.

There were virtually no sanitation facilities for the refugees and they were forced to urinate and defecate where they sat. With temperatures reaching the mid-30s Celcius during the day, the Dutch gathered towels soaked in water and spread them among the refugees as a basic means of freshening themselves up. The stench of sweat and excrement rapidly became unbearable. Fearing that an epidemic might break out the next day, when temperatures were sure to soar again, and anticipating that dehydration and exhaustion would rapidly lead to deaths among the refugees, the next morning the Dutch dug a large hole to serve as a mass grave. Clearly the situation was untenable, and a speedy evacuation of the refugees seemed the only possible solution.

The refugees believed that the Dutch would protect them from the invading 'Četniks' and arrange for them to be taken to safety, but in this expectation they were sorely disappointed. Nor did the Dutch succeed in securing a safe evacuation. Including the soldiers who had retreated from Srebrenica, there were just over 350 Dutch soldiers in Potočari. Overwhelmed by the enormity of the crisis, without clear instructions for dealing with such an emergency, the Dutch battalion struggled to improvise. The Serbs, on the other hand, were acting on the basis of a carefully prepared plan. By the time the Dutch realized this, the deportation of the Muslim population was well under way.

Following the actual seizure of Srebrenica town, the next step in the Serb operation was to concentrate all the refugees in one area, in order to make it easier to deport them. From the beginning, the Serbs planned to separate the men and the boys from the main body of refugees. The women, children and elderly would be transported to Kladanj in Bosnian government-held territory, the men to detention centres in and around Bratunac. As a formality the men would be screened for 'war crimes'. In fact, all of the men were to be executed.

Early reports, on 11 July 1995, from Dutch soldiers in OP Pappa, which was located in the north of the enclave between Potočari and Bratunac, anticipated the fate of the Muslim men:

> Two trucks with forty to fifty male prisoners each, were seen moving in the direction of Bratunac. Soon after these trucks had passed round the bend at Yellow Bridge, a number of salvos were heard, totalling around one hundred shots.[2]

The Serbs knew that the key to a successful deportation was speed. They had to make sure the operation was executed quickly enough to stymie any effective UN response. This required a level of organization and planning just as complicated as that for the actual military operation.

For a start, if the deportation was to run smoothly, sufficient transport capacity had to be assembled. In the end some forty to sixty buses and trucks were used. In Serb-held Bosnia, it was not easy to collect this number of vehicles. What is more, the vehicles needed fuel, which was difficult to come by in an area hit by worldwide sanctions. When officially debriefed in the Netherlands, one Dutch soldier reported that a Serb soldier had told him that the Serbs 'could have executed the military operation one week earlier but had waited until there was sufficient transport capacity to deport the refugees'.[3]

The Serbs paid attention to detail, sending in a fire brigade truck to distribute water among the refugees and also a small truck with bread. A Serb camera team was positioned to record the proceedings.

Apart from logistics, speed depended on the quality of the troops. The units carrying out the deportations and executions had to be efficient and experienced 'ethnic cleansers'. The cooperation of local militia and police, who would be able to help identify and detain suspected Muslim 'war criminals', was also a key. In all, in and around the enclave of Srebrenica, several thousand Serb troops were needed to mop up the enclave, to deport the women and children, and to arrest, detain, interrogate and execute the men.

The third ingredient to a successful operation was to reduce the resistance from both the Dutch and the refugees themselves. To force compliance, the Serbs employed a combination of threats and blandishments. The Dutch were intimidated with token aggression, but at the same time they were told that they would not be harmed if they cooperated. The Muslims were initially reassured by the distribution of some food and water and by promises that they would soon be free to go, provided they gave up their arms and allowed themselves to be screened for war crimes, but they were also subjected to outbursts of indiscriminate violence. Fearful and confused, both groups largely played into the hands of the Serbs.

General Ratko Mladić personally took command of the situation in Potočari on 11 July, soon after his troops had invaded Srebrenica and the enclave had effectively fallen. In the early evening, Lieutenant-Colonel Karremans, as he later told the judges of the War Crimes

Tribunal in The Hague, received a message that he 'had to show up in Bratunac for a meeting' at 20.30.

Upon their arrival at Hotel Fontana in Bratunac, Karremans and the two liaison officers he had brought as an escort found General Mladić waiting. According to an apocryphal story, they were confronted with the scene of a Serb soldier slitting the throat of a pig. Mladić reportedly told the officers 'that was how he would treat people like those protected by the Dutch peacekeepers'.[4] The meeting lasted forty-five minutes. Although Karremans was able to 'explain the poor situation of the refugees', Mladić did most of the talking. Standing with his hands on his hips and elbows turned outwards, he launched into repeated tirades, accusing Karremans of being responsible for the failure to disarm the Muslims, for the bombing of his tanks and for the death of some of his soldiers. He proclaimed that his artillery commanded the compound and threatened to shell the Dutch and the refugees if there were any more attacks by NATO aircraft.

When Mladić finished, Karremans politely replied that Mladić was wrong to accuse him of responsibility for the air attacks. Filmed by a Serb camera crew, he said:

> No, again, that is not decided by me, nor asked for. That is something that they [the UN] offer. They make the decisions on what information I put from the bottom to, let's say, even the UN in New York.

Karremans was twisting the truth and Mladić knew it. The Dutchman's fumbling answer exemplified the psychological dominance Mladić had swiftly established over the Dutch battalion commander.

During the meeting, Karremans and his fellow officers were filmed apparently toasting Mladić's victory. Although Karremans later explained that he had only been holding a glass of water, the effect of the images was to portray the UN and the Dutch army as legitimators of ethnic cleansing. The pictures became a symbol of the UN's humiliation in Srebrenica.

Before leaving Hotel Fontana, the Dutch were told to return a few hours later with a representative from the Muslim refugees. Back in the compound, they 'desperately' began searching for Nesib Mandžić, the respected headmaster of Srebrenica's secondary school. When Mandžić was found, it was explained to him that the situation was 'very serious', both for the Dutch and the refugees. Karremans believed that negotiations could provide the only possible way out. He asked whether Mandžić was prepared to negotiate with the Serbs on behalf of the Bosnians. A year later, Mandžić explained to reporters from Holland's VPRO Television why he had agreed:

> Karremans and other officers promised they would support me in trying to achieve a safe evacuation from the enclave. These were the conditions under which I began to negotiate. They would back up my demands completely.[5]

Together with Mandžić and the two liaison officers, Karremans returned to Hotel Fontana at around 23.45 on 11 July. In his testimony to the War Crimes Tribunal in The Hague, he described the second meeting as a 'little bit friendlier'. Mladić allowed Karremans some time to express his concern for the plight of the refugees and the need for a speedy evacuation of the wounded. Then the Serb general began to talk. He announced that there would be a ceasefire, something Karremans had requested, until 10.00 the following morning. By that time Karremans must return to Bratunac with a delegation of Muslim officials. Mladić told Karremans and Mandžić that all Muslim soldiers in Potočari should lay down their arms if they were to be given free passage to Bosnian government-held territory. According to Karremans, Mladić warned: 'If they should keep their weapons, that will be their death.'

Karremans felt that he had few, if any, options. Before the two meetings with Mladić, he had received instructions from the acting UNPROFOR commander in Sarajevo, French General Hervé Gobilliard, 'to take all reasonable measures to protect refugees and civilians in [his] care' and to 'defend [his] forces'. Karremans received the instructions via the Sector Command in Tuzla, where Karremans' direct superior, Dutch Colonel Charlef Brantz, had first read them and twice scribbled 'not possible' in the margins of the document. The colonel knew that the instructions had already been overtaken by events.

In the early morning of 12 July, following the two meetings with Mladić, Karremans sent a fax to the Sector Command in Tuzla, to UNPROFOR Command in Sarajevo, to the Command in Zagreb and to the Dutch Ministry of Defence in The Hague. He emphasized that he was not able effectively to defend either the refugees or his own battalion and said:

> The situation is deteriorating in such [a] way that additional measures must be taken for both refugees and soldiers. In my opinion there is one way out: negotiations today at the highest level.

Some high-level contacts were in fact explored that day. The US chargé d'affaires in Belgrade, Rudolph Perina, met President Milošević and warned him that the fall of Srebrenica was a serious blow to the 'peace process'. He urged the Serbian president to 'cut off all military supplies' to the Bosnian Serbs. Milošević coldly replied that he was 'stung' by the US *démarche*, asking, 'Why blame me? I have been unable to contact Mladić.' He told Perina that 'he had been assured that Bosnian Serb forces would not harm UN peacekeepers or Muslim civilians'.[6] But he did not speculate on what lay in store for the Muslim men.

Both UNPF commander General Janvier and the Dutch government tried to bring more senior officials and officers into Potočari to take over direct talks with Mladić. But as General Nicolai reported to The Hague from Sarajevo, on the morning of 13 July, 'Mladić exclusively wants to do business with Ton Karremans.'[7] Mladić was clearly satisfied with the way events were unfolding and was not interested in jeopardizing their course. Karremans was on his own.

At 10.30 on Wednesday 12 July, Karremans and his two liaison officers met with Mladić for the third time. They were accompanied by a delegation of four Bosnians, who had been asked to represent the refugees. One of them was Čamila Purković. She later told VPRO Television about an exchange she had had with Mladić during the meeting:

> Mladić said to me: 'Do you think that the Dutch are afraid of me? I don't fear them. I am stronger than all of you. They cannot protect you.' I said: 'I know that, there are too few of them. Do as you like.'

By this time, the UN and the Dutch government had agreed that Dutchbat should 'monitor the evacuation of the refugees', and Karremans had been informed of this before the meeting. The decision, however necessary, played into Mladić's hands by allowing him to dictate his own terms for the evacuation virtually unchallenged. The first evacuation, to Kladanj, was to begin at 13.00, and its escort would be the Bosnian Serb Army. The refugees were to be divided into five groups, the first four being the wounded, the weak and infirm, women and children, and Dutchbat and the international staff. The fifth group, the Muslim men, would be screened in an interrogation centre for possible involvement in war crimes. The UN was to provide all fuel for the refugee transports.

Nesib Mandžić and Ibro Nuhanović, two of the other Muslim representatives, protested against the separation of the men. Karremans seconded their objection and told Mladić, 'if there is to be an evacuation . . . my own battalion should be its escort.' He proposed to put a Dutch soldier on every vehicle.

A year later, reflecting on what had happened in Potočari, Karremans wrote, 'During the third meeting, on Wednesday morning 12 July 1995, it became clear that Mladić was operating entirely according to a pre-planned scenario.'[8] Reporting back to Voorhoeve after the meeting, Karremans told him of Mladić's intention to separate the men from the women, which clearly was going to entail serious risks for the men. Voorhoeve directly instructed Karremans 'not to assist in any way with the ethnic cleansing and the separation of men and women'. He added, rather ambiguously, that Karremans should 'see to it that the forced evacuation takes place in as humane a way as possible'.[9]

The Bosnian and Dutchbat delegations returned to the compound shortly after noon. Shortly thereafter, the Bosnians were informed by the Dutch deputy battalion commander, Major Franken, that they were now officially the 'refugees representatives working group'. Distributing pens and notepads, he explained that their main task was to draw up an evacuation plan for the 25,000 refugees from Potočari. The Bosnians started immediately. But as they worked, Serb buses and trucks, which were operating on a completely different agenda, began to arrive.

The first Serb soldiers walked into Potočari between 11.00 and 12.00 on 12 July. They came from the direction of Bratunac, in the north, which was remarkable since over the past six days the main line of attack had been from the south. The shift indicated that the assignment of the soldiers who had carried out the actual military operation had ended. They had been withdrawn and probably sent towards Žepa, which came under Serb artillery fire from 11 July and was attacked on 14 July.

The Serb soldiers who arrived in Potočari that Wednesday demanded immediate entry to the Dutch compound. They insisted on their right to inspect the refugees. Initially, the peacekeepers refused to open the gate, but the Serbs threatened to use force if necessary and were finally let in. Five Serbs made a brief tour of the compound and left. Meanwhile a growing number of Serb soldiers and military police were flooding into the area. All that stood between the Serbs and the refugees was a thin blue line of Dutch peacekeepers.

Shortly after the arrival of the soldiers, a small Serb truck arrived, laden with bread. A Dutch soldier reflected afterwards:

> As a propaganda stunt bread was being distributed by the Bosnian Serbs everywhere and was eagerly accepted by the hungry masses. But a request by the BSA to stage such a scene within the compound and film it was denied.[10]

The Serb camera team did manage to film outside the compound, however, and as they were doing so, a Serb fire-brigade truck arrived and distributed water among the refugees. Some Serb soldiers handed out sweets. The Muslims were given a false sense of hope. They advanced towards the Serbs, putting pressure on the Dutch cordon. Their sense of relief was reinforced by the words of Mladić himself, who arrived while the bread and water were being distributed.

Brushing aside the protests of Dutch Lieutenant Koster, Mladić, filmed by his own camera crew, reassured the Muslims:

> All who wish to go will be transported, large and small, young and old. Don't be afraid, just take it easy. Let the women and children go first. Thirty buses will come and take you in the direction of Kladanj. No one will harm you.

Lieutenant Koster came up to Mladić again, insisting that he should speak first with Karremans before saying any more. This irritated Mladić, who replied on camera, 'It will be done according to my orders. I don't care about your commander.'

While Serb buses were pulling up on the road next to the compound, Koster for the third time demanded to know from Mladić what his plans were. Mladić answered that he was going to transport the refugees to a better location and that nobody was going to stop him. As the lieutenant was reporting this to his superiors back in the compound, the Serbs pushed aside some of the Dutch soldiers, and the desperate Muslims began to stream toward the buses. Koster later wrote:

> The situation, as far as we were able to control it at all, was now taken out of our hands altogether. It was incomprehensible; a large part of the refugees pushed forward in order to be transported, another part refused.[11]

The first buses with refugees left at about 15.00. In the initial pandemonium some Muslim men managed to make it on to the buses. But the Serbs quickly stopped this and began to separate them from their families. The men were taken to a house south-west of the compound, where they were guarded by soldiers and policemen with Alsatian dogs. Their personal possessions were taken from them and burnt. Later, they too were put on buses, but they were driven to Bratunac instead of Kladanj.

These buses returned empty to Potočari within the hour to take away more men. When the Dutch began to realize that Muslim men were being deported separately, they tried to follow the convoys. But as soon as they reached the outskirts of Bratunac, Serb soldiers stopped them, while the buses with the men drove on. Over the next few days, Dutch soldiers held hostage in Bratunac reported seeing a number of buses filled with male prisoners. Most of the men sat with their heads between their knees, and when they did look up their expressions were of terror. The Dutch hostages also reported hearing frequent gunshots, particularly from the direction of the football pitch.

Several of the hostages noticed that Serb military police would leave Bratunac for the former 'safe area' between 07.00 and 08.00 every morning and return in the evening exhausted. Some of the Serbs chatted to the Dutch. Johan Bos, a 31-year old sergeant, was quoted in the *Independent on Sunday* on 23 July 1995:

They bragged about how they had murdered people and raped women. They were proud of what they were doing. I didn't get the feeling they were doing it out of anger or revenge, more for fun. They seemed pleased with themselves in a sort of professional, low-key way. I believed what they said, because they looked and behaved as if they were more than capable of doing what they claimed. Each had an Alsatian dog, a gun, handcuffs and a terrifying-looking knife with a blade about 9 ins. long.

When Karremans saw that the Serbs were using up to sixty buses and trucks, he concluded that he could not put a Dutch soldier on every vehicle. Instead he decided to escort each convoy with two Dutch Mercedes jeeps, each manned by a Dutch officer and driver. Initially, some Dutch escort vehicles made it to the drop-off point near Kladanj together with the convoys. Then the Serbs began confiscating the vehicles. In the end none of the Dutch jeeps returned to Potočari; in one afternoon fourteen were taken. The soldiers from the escorts were held by the Serbs at a number of points along the route 'for their own safety'. The Serbs did not want the Dutch to witness what was happening on the road between Kladanj and Bratunac.

A seven-vehicle convoy with over fifty wounded people left Potočari at 18.00 on 12 July. Apart from the wounded, the convoy also contained some Dutchbat personnel and ten young Muslim women working for the international humanitarian organization Médécins sans Frontières (MSF). Upon arrival at the drop-off point near Kladanj, the Serb soldiers initially were friendly. But when they discovered men of fighting age among the wounded, their attitude abruptly changed. They ordered twenty wounded to get out of the vehicles and walk to Kladanj. From the drop-off point, Kladanj was still another six kilometres away, and some of the wounded could only crawl. A 19-year old MSF assistant was taken off as well. She returned to the bus some time later, greatly distressed, saying that she had been raped by three Serbs.

In the evening of 12 July the deportation stopped. Already there were indications that Serbs were picking men out of the crowd of refugees and executing them. That afternoon, a number of Dutch soldiers saw a group of at least five Muslim men being forced by the

Serbs to enter a big factory hall opposite the compound. A little while later they heard five or six gunshots. After some time they saw a Serb, armed with a pistol, come out of the building. The Dutch soldiers believed the Muslims had been murdered, but for reasons of safety they were unable to investigate immediately. Later, they found no evidence of an execution.[12]

Around the compound refugees watched in terror as Serb soldiers entered the factory halls and took away men and young boys, claiming they were looking for war criminals. One Bosnian woman later told Human Rights Watch:

> By that night, the people who hadn't been transported yet became hysterical and frightened. We began to hear talk about corpses being discovered in the area . . . By Thursday morning, women were wailing and crying because many of their husbands and/or sons had been taken away by the Četniks for one reason or another, but had not been brought back.[13]

Another witness account to Human Rights Watch came from a Bosnian Muslim mother who had taken refuge in one of the factories with her son.

> The Četniks came into the building wearing camouflage police uniforms with the *kokarda*[14] on their caps, and they started taking boys out of the building. They took about thirty boys away, we don't know where, but we never saw them again . . . We didn't dare look too closely [lest we drew] attention to ourselves. I was hiding my son. That night while we were in the building, we could hear screaming from outside – terrible screams all around, and the women were all crying for their sons. My son and I spent that night together terrified. He said we shouldn't wait another day to leave – that we should leave tomorrow.[15]

When Nesib Mandžić was informed by civilians that executions had taken place during the night, in desperation he asked Major Franken to stop the evacuation. Franken responded that he would do everything he could. But the deportation continued. Now acutely worried about the fate of the men, Franken gave instructions to make a list of all Muslim males of draft-age, hoping this would enhance their security by enabling the UN to check on their whereabouts at a later stage.

This only succeeded on the compound, and even there only partially. A list was compiled of 239 men, with some sixty more refusing to put their names on it.

The deportations resumed at 06.30 on 13 July. By now extremely frightened, the refugees were desperate to get away from the factory halls and reach what they hoped would be the relative safety of the buses. But once there, the women again witnessed their husbands, brothers, sons and grandsons being dragged away and assembled into a separate group.

Zoran Petrović, a Serb cameraman from Belgrade, had arrived on the scene and recorded the separation of men and women, as Serb soldiers yelled,

> Follow the line! Behind him! No, No! You lot to the left, in a column one by one.

Hurem Suljić, a 55-year-old carpenter with a withered leg, believed the Serbs would allow him to leave together with his family. But when they reached the buses, he was separated from his wife, daughter, daughter-in-law and seven-year-old granddaughter, as he told BBC's *Panorama*:

> As I got there someone grabbed me by the shoulder and said: 'You, old man, go up there to the end of the road. You can't leave now.' I said: 'I can't separate from my family. How will I ever find them again?' He said: 'Don't talk back. Go to the left.'

Clearly the Serbs were not just hunting down able-bodied men of draft-age. Suljić was taken to the white house and held there with other Muslim men.

> So I walked over to the left . . . there was a group of people standing there, and when the group got bigger they told us all to go to a house about ten to fifteen metres away from the road. They told us to go into the house and sit down.

The Dutch soldiers and the small team of UN monitors were growing increasingly anxious about what was taking place inside the house. One of the UN monitors, Kenyan Major Joseph Kingori, was filmed by Petrović, saying:

I'm talking about the overcrowding in that place. Where all the men have been taken is too crowded. They are sitting on each other — it's not good.

Two Dutch soldiers were allowed to enter the house where the men were being held to bring them some water. They secretly took pictures of the men, who, as one of them later reported, were 'gripped by a deadly fear'. According to Suljić, General Mladić came to inspect the men that afternoon.

He [Mladić] came to the door of the house where we were sitting, he looked in and said, 'Hello neighbours.' Some people greeted him back. 'Do you know me?' he asked. Some said yes, some were quiet. He introduced himself as Ratko Mladić. 'If you didn't know me before, now you have the chance to see me,' he said. 'Do you see now what your Government has done to you? It has abandoned you. It wouldn't protect you, even NATO cannot protect you. It's all in vain because we are not afraid of anybody. You thought that Srebrenica would never fall,' he said, 'but we will take Srebrenica when we like.'

That same afternoon, Lieutenant Koster was informed by two fellow soldiers of rumours that nine Muslim men had been executed. The soldiers had a vague idea where the bodies might be, and Koster decided to accompany them to the site. He later gave a chilling description of what they found:

They lay almost in a line on the ground. Dressed in civilian clothes, lying on their stomachs and with a gunshot entry wound in the middle of their back. A number of identity papers were lying around close to the bodies and we decided to take these with us.[16]

The Serbs naturally tried to hide human-rights violations from the Dutch and were mostly successful in doing so. None the less Koster now had irrefutable proof that the Serbs had committed summary executions of Muslim men. He asked one of the soldiers to take pictures for evidence.[17]

Medic Richard van Duuren belonged to a group of Dutch who decided on 13 July to drive into Srebrenica town and see if there were any elderly people remaining who they might take back to Potočari.

> Near a small roundabout [in Srebrenica], I saw three bodies. One lay quite far away, the second was lying next to the roundabout and the third I saw from very close up. This body had already turned black (it was over 40 degrees Celsius) and there was a big pool of dried blood near his mouth. It was clear the man had been executed, because he was still sitting on his knees, even though he had fallen sideways. He had been shot, either through the back of his head, or through his mouth. We drove on and [eventually found] five to six old people, whom we put in the truck and took back with us to Potočari.

One Dutchman actually witnessed a Muslim man being murdered. At around 16.00 on 13 July Corporal Paul Groenewegen saw a group of four Serbs pull a man out of a crowd of refugees and force him to walk to the corner of a house. The man was ordered to stand with his face to the wall and was shot through the back of his head with an AK-47. In his testimony to the Tribunal in The Hague, Groenewegen remembered hearing twenty to forty single shots per hour being fired all day. He told the BBC's *Panorama* that he believed this indicated executions had been taking place on a systematic basis. Groenewegen's account was echoed by Christina Schmitz, a German nurse working for MSF. She reported hearing regular 'shots from handguns' from behind the house where the men were detained.[18]

The refugees outside the Dutch compound were desperate to get away from Potočari and so more often than not did not hinder the efficiency of the Serb operation. By 16.00 on 13 July all the refugees outside the compound had been deported. It was now time for the refugees within the compound to leave. The Bosnians inside the compound had been asking the Dutch all day what would happen to the men. But the Dutch had been reluctant to answer. According to one of the UN interpreters, Major Franken attempted to calm the refugees by recounting an exchange with the Serbs:

> I showed them [the Serbs] the list [with the 239 Muslim men] and told them that I have already sent it to the Dutch

government and to Geneva and to some more addresses by fax. They were not very happy about it. I think that they would think twice before they do something bad to the men. That is all I can do for the men at the moment. Anyway, I will hide a copy of the list in my underwear.[19]

Yet of the 239 names on the list of men, at least 103 definitely appear on the Red Cross list of missing men from Srebrenica but it is likely that over two thirds are missing.[20] Following Major Franken's brief words, the Dutch asked three of the interpreters to warn the refugees that they were about to be evacuated. Standing on vehicles they addressed their fellow Bosnians, repeating verbatim the words they were given by the Dutch. One of the interpreters later accused the Dutch of having kept the truth about what was happening outside the compound from the refugees within it.

[First] they said, 'Tell them they have to start leaving the camp.' Their second sentence was, 'Men can go with their families.'[21]

It took only three hours to deport the refugees from the compound itself. By 19.00 on 13 July all Muslim refugees had left the compound. The Srebrenica enclave was ethnically clean.

In The Hague, meanwhile, the Dutch government was working out the 'modalities of a possible departure of Dutchbat'. These 'modalities' had been discussed that morning between the chief of defence staff, General Henk van den Breemen, and by General Cees Nicolai in Sarajevo.

At 18.00 on 13 July, General Nicolai faxed an instruction, in Dutch, on the 'negotiations between C[ommanding] O[fficer] Dutchbat and Mladić about evacuation Dutchbat *cum suis* (MSF, UNHCR, Local employees)'. Points 6, 8 and 9 of the instructions read:

6. Take locals in the service of the UN with you.
8. If negotiations get stuck, refer back immediately to BGen Nicolai (plenipotentiary negotiator on behalf of NL government and UNPROFOR).
9. Threats are, for the time being, to be ignored robustly and immediately reported, irrespective of the time of day.

By the time Nicolai's message reached Dutchbat HQ, point 6 was moot: the local UN employees were already gone. The Dutchbat command had decided that, apart from the refugee representatives, only those employees who possessed UN accreditation could be evacuated together with the Dutch. This meant the six Bosnian interpreters. The cleaning ladies, laundry women, kitchen aids, the electrician, the plumber and the two garbage collectors were all excluded. The hairdresser did possess UN accreditation, but he had been spotted in uniform during the battle for Srebrenica: very much against the rules. The remaining local employees had been selected by the Srebrenica Presidency rather than the UN and thus 'sub-contracted', as it were, to Dutchbat. According to the decision of Dutchbat (which seemed to contradict the instruction by General Nicolai), they did not qualify to be evacuated together with the Dutch themselves.

Hasan Nuhanović was one of the six interpreters. His father, Ibro, was one of the refugee representatives. As such, both men had permission to stay and leave together with the Dutch. But neither Hasan's younger brother nor his mother possessed a UN pass. When the interpreter found out that an evacuation list had been typed that did not include them, he pleaded with the Dutch officers to at least put his brother, who seemed in imminent danger, on it. They refused. At around 18.00 on 13 July, when nearly all the refugees had left the compound, the Nuhanović family were told by the Dutch that they had to go. The family walked to the gate. Hasan wanted to leave with his family, but his screaming brother insisted that he should stay inside the compound. Ibro, the father, decided to accompany his wife and son. Just before leaving the compound, he kissed Major Franken in a desperate attempt to convince the Serbs he had a close relationship with the Dutch. But ten metres outside the compound the Serbs separated the two men from their wife and mother. Hasan stood, forlorn, just inside the entrance. A year later, all three members of his family were still missing.

Standing at the gate, Hasan was spotted by Major Franken. Nuhanović recounted the following exchange for VPRO Television:

> Franken asked me, 'Hasan, what are you doing there?' I asked, 'Why?' He said, 'You are not supposed to be here. The Serbs are coming in a couple of minutes to see who is left in the

camp. They will have the list. They will compare it with your identity cards. Run to the bar. The others from the list are already sitting in the bar, waiting for the Serbs.'

Once there, Hasan discovered that MSF, as well as the UN High Commission for Refugees (UNHCR), had been able to place not only their local employees, but also their family members, on the list of evacuees. Nuhanović later bitterly reflected:

> Everyone was afraid. The Dutch were afraid. We were afraid, but I don't know who was more afraid. I think we had much more reason to be afraid than the Dutch. As far as I know, the Dutch all arrived home safely.

(In the end the Serbs only paid the compound a brief visit. Repelled by the stench left by the refugees, they did not check the identity cards. On 19 July they gave official permission for the local employees to leave together with the Dutch.)

In Tuzla, Colonel Brantz was worried. By the evening of 13 July, he had detected a shortfall of 4,000 Muslim men. Either there had been a miscount or something had happened to the men on the way from Potočari to Tuzla. Brantz reported the discrepancy to the UNPF command in Zagreb. He tried to impress upon his superiors that 'timely action might prevent the violation of human rights'. Akashi included Brantz's concerns in his written report to New York on 14 July. But by then it was too late.

In the meantime, while the refugees were being deported, the Dutch government had devoted much attention to arranging the evacuation of its own troops from Serb-held Bosnia. Dutch Foreign Minister Hans van Mierlo asked his German colleague, Klaus Kinkel, to intercede with Russian Foreign Minister Andrei Kozyrev and ask him to use his 'good contacts' with Serbia and the Bosnian Serbs to negotiate the release of the Dutch hostages held in Bratunac and Simići.[22] Kozyrev dispatched his experienced negotiator Vitaly Churkin, who arrived in Pale on Friday 14 July. There he met with the Bosnian Serb leadership and quickly secured the release of the Dutch hostages.

On 15 July, with the operation against Srebrenica nearing completion, General Mladić arrived in Belgrade for a secret meeting with

Serbian President Slobodan Milošević, EU mediator Carl Bildt and a reluctant UNPROFOR commander Lieutenant-General Rupert Smith, who had returned from leave.

The Belgrade meeting confirmed that the Dutch hostages could be released. (Indeed, they left Serb-held Bosnia the same day.) It was also agreed that the whole of Dutchbat would be allowed to leave on 21 July. From Mladić's point of view this was important: it meant he would have a substantial number of 'hostages' for another week. He could use this time, during which the UN would be reluctant to use air power against his troops, to seize Žepa.

It was also agreed that the Red Cross would gain access to the captured Muslim men. Finally, Mladić demanded that UNPRO-FOR should compensate him for the fuel he had used to 'evacuate' the Muslims from Potočari. Smith refused, none the less, that same day 30,000 litres of fuel were delivered by Dutchbat to the Serbs in Bratunac.

On 17 July, in another example of the Serb desire for public-relations legitimacy, Miroslav Deronjić, the new Serbian 'Civil Affairs Commissioner for Srebrenica', visited the Dutch compound in Potočari with a document stating that the evacuation had been carried out correctly. Deronjić wanted Major Franken and Nesib Mandžić to sign it. Mandžić later commented:

> When Mr Franken and I had read this document we looked at each other in silence. Without words we understood that the document did not correspond to the truth.

But the Bosnian and the Dutchman had no choice. Mandžić signed it. Franken did too, adding the handwritten remark that the operation had been carried out correctly 'as far as it concerns convoys actually escorted by UN forces'.

The Dutch left on 21 July. By then, the other east Bosnian enclave, Žepa, had also fallen to the Serbs. The Dutch equipment confiscated by the Serbs had not been returned. The Red Cross had not been allowed to visit any Muslim prisoners. It had taken the Serbs just thirty hours to deport 23,000 people, virtually all women and children, from Potočari to Kladanj, where they were in a position of relative safety. The Serbs had also taken as many as 1,700 men to Bratunac. Theirs was an entirely different fate.

NOTES

1. Lieutenant E. Koster, 'Opvang vluchtelingen' ('Refugee relief'), in *Dutchbat in Vredesnaam*, p. 321.
2. *Debriefing*, p. 52.
3. *Debriefing*, p. 60.
4. Stephen Kinzer, 'Dutch conscience stung by troops' Bosnia failure', *New York Times*, 8 October 1995. The Dutch noticed a pig being slaughtered during their second, midnight meeting, but Mladić did not accompany this with a comment.
5. *Lopende Zaken*, VPRO Television, 23 June 1996.
6. Michael Dobbs and R. Jeffrey Smith, 'New proof offered of Serb atrocities', *Washington Post*, 29 October 1995.
7. Henk van den Breemen, 'Hollands Dagboek' ('Dutch Diary'), *NRC/Handelsblad*, 22 July 1995.
8. *Dutchbat in Vredesnaam*, p. 334.
9. *Handelingen Tweede Kamer, 1994–1995 (Parliamentary Proceedings)*, 22 181, No. 109, 27 July 1995.
10. *Dutchbat in Vredesnaam*, p. 313.
11. *Dutchbat in Vredesnaam*, p. 323.
12. *Debriefing*, p. 50.
13. Human Rights Watch/Helsinki, 'Bosnia-Hercegovina: The fall of Srebrenica and the failure of UN peacekeeping', Vol. 7, No. 13 (October 1995), p. 19.
14. A Serbian nationalist symbol, depicting a double-headed eagle, worn by some paramilitary groups.
15. Human Rights Watch/Helsinki, 'The fall of Srebrenica', p. 19.
16. *Dutchbat in Vredesnaam*, p. 324.
17. The film which contained the pictures of the nine bodies also had pictures of the prisoners in the house. The film was accidentally destroyed while being developed by the Dutch Ministry of Defence.
18. Bob van Laerhoven, *Srebrenica: Getuigen van een massamoord (Srebrenica: Witnesses to a Mass Murder)* (Antwerp: Icarus, 1996), p. 141.
19. Letter from Hasan Nuhanović to the 'Members of the [Netherlands] Permanent Parliamentary Commission for Foreign Affairs', 30 October 1995.
20. According to the Red Cross, the names and dates of birth of 116 men from the Dutch list of 239 correspond exactly to the details on the Red Cross list of missing people. Of these 116, 103 are said to be missing, seven are said to have arrived in central Bosnia, and five were found by

the Red Cross in prison in Batković. Fifty of the remaining names did not occur in the Red Cross files. Another sixty-five names of missing men were the same as on the Dutch list, but had different dates of birth; two names were spelt slightly differently. The remaining three names corresponded, but the Red Cross doubted whether they concerned the same people. *Handelingen Tweede Kamer, 1995–1996*, 22 181, No. 134, 30 November 1995, p. 23.

21. *Lopende Zaken*, VPRO Television, 14 April 1996.
22. Syp Wynia, 'Nederlandse VN'ers danken vrijlating aan de Russen' ('Dutch UN troops owe release to Russians'), *Het Parool*, 18 July 1995.

CHAPTER THREE

The Massacre

The video images have become familiar. A Serb soldier, standing on a road flanked by hilly woodlands, yells out, 'Come on guys. Out with you!' The camera veers to the left. The silhouette of a line of men, walking over a ridge, comes into view. 'You see! There is a whole lot of people.' The first soldier speaks with Zoran Petrović, the Serb cameraman from Belgrade:

> 'About fifteen of them have gone through.'
> 'How many have come out so far?'
> 'It must be three to four thousand, for sure.'
> 'And they have all surrendered to you here?'
> 'Yes.'

One of the next scenes is of a group of men huddled together in collective terror. It is a brief final image of some of the thousands of Muslim men from Srebrenica who were captured by the Serbs and who have never been seen alive again.

On Tuesday 12 July, the last of Srebrenica's Muslim defenders fell back to the hills to the west and north-west of Srebrenica. They had failed to force the UN to intervene on their behalf, and their battle was clearly lost. From the vantage of the hills, they watched the Serbs enter the town. The defence secretary of the Srebrenica enclave, Suljo Hasanović, had left the town shortly after 14.00, along with other members of the Presidency. From the hills around the hamlet of Kutlići, they witnessed the NATO air attack on Serb tanks near the transmitter tower:

> It was two planes. They dropped some bombs on Serb forces. But it was not real bombs; they were practice bombs . . . There

were another two planes. That was all the help we got. It was then that we understood we had been sold by the international community.

Around this time there were heated debates about whether the men should try to escape to Žepa or, alternatively, to central Bosnia. Getting to Žepa would be difficult because the main Serb attacking force blocked the way. Also a (false) rumour had spread that Žepa had fallen. So central Bosnia was finally chosen. The specific route, which was more quickly decided on, would take the men north-west in the direction of Konjević Polje and Cerska and then further north, past Zvornik, to Križevići. Once there, they would have to choose a point to cross into Bosnian-held territory. This route had a number of advantages over the alternative one due west of the enclave, which was very mountainous and which also ran past one of the main Serb army bases in Bosnia in Vlasenica. The chosen route, on the other hand, would take the men through territory once controlled by the Muslims and which was known to many who had lived there and ended up as refugees in Srebrenica. Tension was unbearably high, and there was much in-fighting between the Muslims. The Dutch troops in OP Mike, which was just outside Jaglići, described the situation among the Bosnians as 'chaotic'. On Monday night, as the Serbs were closing in, the Dutch witnessed a passionate dispute over whether to abandon or defend the enclave. On the Tuesday night, the Bosnians fought again. The Dutch, meanwhile, had decided that they wanted to abandon their post. A local Bosnian commander gave his 'permission' for the Dutch to leave if they agreed to take his wife and children with them to Potočari. However, some Bosnian soldiers disagreed with this decision to let the Dutch withdraw, and when they began to do so, a Bosnian aimed his anti-tank weapon at the Dutch YPR. Fearing for the safety of his wife and children, the Bosnian commander shot his own man at close range through the head.

On the night of 11–12 July, between 10,000 and 15,000 men (and a few women and children, mostly families of the senior military), who had converged on the area of Jaglići and Šušnjari, prepared to leave. Attempts were made to organize the mass of men into some sort of a column. The plan was to put the regular soldiers in the vanguard so that they could break through the Serb lines and open up a corridor for the rest. In the dark, the men anxiously waited for those in front of them to start moving. The trick would be to move as quickly as possible while at the same time following carefully in the steps of those marching ahead, in order to avoid the minefields just outside the enclave. So many people had crowded the area that it took many hours before they could all depart. The first groups set off at midnight, but by midday men were still leaving. Like a long snake, the column stretched for miles through the hills.

The regular soldiers in the front made speedy progress. There was some shelling, but the Serbs did not put up serious opposition. Defence Secretary Hasanović, who had left with the first group at midnight, covered the twenty-five kilometres or so to the Konjević Polje area in six hours. There, he remembered, his group paused to rest. Since they were more vulnerable in daylight, they planned to continue their march at the end of the day. For the moment, they were relatively safe. The Serbs had decided not to pick a fight, yet, with the strongest element in the column.

But the less-professional soldiers and civilians who followed were not so fortunate. The Serbs sprung their trap swiftly.[1] At the very beginning, they let the men move along without too much incident, knowing that to chase and to catch the men in the thickly forested, mountainous terrain would be difficult. But at some point, the Muslims would have to cross either the Bratunac–Konjevići road, north of the enclave, or the Konjevići–Milići road, to the west. And this is where the Serbs waited. Soldiers, reinforced by armoured vehicles and anti-aircraft machine guns, lined the roads at ten- to twenty-metre intervals. All the Serbs had to do was exercise patience and wait for the Muslims to show up. During the early hours of the morning, the Serb soldiers north of the hamlet of Kamenica noticed large numbers of men approaching. To scare them out, artillery, mortars and the anti-aircraft guns opened fire on the woods along the roads.

After the ten-kilometre trek towards Kamenica, the Muslims hesitated when they realized the Serbs were patrolling the road in front of them. They did not know what to do next. One of the refugees remembered the harrowing scene:

We stayed there for the rest of the day and the night. After a while, we realized that we had to move, one way or another, or else we were surely dead. The Serbs knew this too, so they just waited. They had squeezed everyone into one small spot near Kamenica. After we walked about 500 metres, the Serbs began shooting everywhere. I remember a tree falling down and killing more than twenty people at one point.[2]

Unable to escape northwards, the men were driven west along the Bratunac–Konjevići road, toward Nova Kasaba. By then the column had lost all cohesion:

Serb tanks were placed all along the route from Kravica to Konjević Polje up to the intersection at Konjević Polje. My brother and I saw people falling down. Dead and wounded were all around. We were simply running without knowing where we were going. One shell fell near me, and I was terrified. That's when my brother and I separated. I haven't seen him since.

The Serbs on the roads called out to the men to give up and surrender – a demand the desperate men found increasingly difficult to resist. Most of them had been on the move for one or more days *prior* to leaving the enclave. Most had not eaten a proper meal for a long time, and few had had time adequately to prepare for the journey and bring sufficient, if any, food. Tired, defenceless and scared, men began to come out of the forest. One survivor told Human Rights Watch:

I saw, about 200 metres in front of me, about 100 people yelling 'Don't shoot! We give up,' and giving themselves up to the Četniks who rounded them up and took them away.[3]

Another testified:

The Četniks started shelling the woods with mortars and calling for us to come out and give up. They told us that they would send the elderly to their families and they would keep the younger men for exchanges.[4]

The combination of fear, lack of food and exhaustion caused great disorientation and confusion, and some men seemed to go temporarily insane. Others could see no way out and committed suicide. The situation grew even worse at night. Among the terrified Muslims fantastic rumours spread. Human Rights Watch collected numerous statements from men who claimed that Serb soldiers in civilian clothes had infiltrated their groups, claiming to know the way to safety. Those who purportedly fell for this ruse were never seen again. Another alleged Serb misdeed was to inject the hapless men with hallucinatory drugs. Witness 'I.N.' claimed that:

> As night fell, we saw groups of men merging into our column. I saw unfamiliar faces; one of them started saying, 'Hurry up with the wounded! Hurry up with the wounded!' All of a sudden we realized that the unfamiliar men were Četniks who had infiltrated our column. There was a lot of them, about 300. They ordered us to leave the injured and wounded at the side of the road, while their men started giving them injections and making them swallow some kind of pills. Later, people who were at the end of our column said that the injured and wounded people looked like they were dying [as a result of the drugs].[5]

Such stories are examples of the degree of fear and exhaustion the men suffered and the paranoia this induced. In some cases, men killed other men whom they did not recognize and suspected of being disguised Serbs.

Yet it is unlikely that Serbs actually infiltrated the groups of Muslims. The pills, the injections or even, as some witnesses allege, the use of gas, were inefficient ways of killing. They also exposed the Serbs to unnecessary risks. How would their own party recognize Serbs in disguise? Who would volunteer to lead unsuspecting Muslims into an ambush? Why inject people or feed them pills, if waiting on the roads for them was so much easier? Dr Ilijas Pilav, one of the few doctors who had worked in the enclave, recalled his own experience:

> A megaphone voice reverberated against the mountainside. The Četniks summoned us to surrender. Escape was impossible, they said. But we did not react and waited until nightfall. The waiting tried our nerves to the utmost. Some people in the group began to hallucinate. Fear. Stress. Such people were a danger to their comrades: they shouted and screamed and could betray our

position to the Četniks. Some armed men completely panicked and opened fire randomly. They shot a few of their own men. We had to overpower them with force.[6]

Several days later, Pilav himself began to hallucinate while crossing through a minefield:

I remember that I was walking, that is, I felt my body walk, but only with a small part of my consciousness. While I was running [through the field], and vaguely conscious of it, I was also sleeping and had crazy, terrible dreams. At one point, I heard my own voice say, 'Enough, when I get some money together, I will buy a car and never walk again, not an inch.' The strange sound of my own voice woke me up.[7]

In places, people were lured out of the forests by Serb soldiers masquerading as UN blue helmets. UN equipment, clothes and vehicles that had been stolen from the Dutch and other UN soldiers were used for the purpose. In one incident two Dutch peacekeepers, who had been removed from a convoy, were taken to somewhere near Konjevići, where they encountered two confiscated YPRs and some eight Serb soldiers in UN uniforms. Ordered to sit in one of the YPRs, they were given a firearm and told that, 'for their own security', if they saw any Bosnian soldiers, they should open fire. Nothing happened, and after a while the men were allowed to return to Potočari. Serb video footage also confirms that the Serbs wore UN equipment and uniforms. How many Muslim men fell for this charade is impossible to tell, but given their desperation, the numbers may have been substantial.

Perhaps the largest group to see indications of Serbian atrocities around Srebrenica were the women and peacekeepers who made up the convoys to Kladanj. They reported seeing large groups of captured Muslim men as well as hundreds of dead bodies. Some of the captured men were spotted being forced by the Serbs to make the three-finger Serb salute. Others had their hands behind or above their heads. Ajkuna Alić told a journalist from *The Times* about what happened after her bus was stopped near Kravica:

'See your army?' [a Serb soldier asked]. Kneeling in the grass were many men I knew. They had their hands behind their necks. I saw one of my sons among them. But I could say nothing to him. I do not know if he saw me.[8]

Neither the Dutch soldiers nor the women noticed any signs of resistance. It appears that the main body of Muslim soldiers had by then already broken through Serb lines and that the Serbs were engaged in a 'mopping up' operation of mainly defenceless civilians and some soldiers.

The Petrović video shows some of the men being captured. One of these was identified by BBC's *Panorama* as Ramo Mustafić. Petrović engaged him in conversation. In answer to an unheard question, Mustafić responded:

> 'We've spent two days and nights here.'
> 'Where are your guns?'
> 'I wasn't carrying a gun. I'm a civilian.'
> 'Are you afraid?'
> 'How can I not be afraid?'

Panorama was unable to trace Mustafić. He appears on the Red Cross list of the missing people from Srebrenica.

From the statements of the few survivors, it is possible to reconstruct how the murder of thousands of captured Muslim men was organized. A substantial number were summarily executed as soon as they surrendered. Those who survived this initial round of indiscriminate killing were taken to collection and interrogation points.

Among Ramo Mustafić's group was a 16-year-old, Enver Husić, who later managed to escape. He was interviewed by BBC's *Panorama*, without having seen the Serb film in which he himself featured:

> Further down, there was a man with a camera, I think he was from CNN. He was filming. A Četnik came along and hit him and said, 'What's he doing here? Get away from here . . .' So we got down and surrendered.
>
> PANORAMA: *Did the man with the camera say anything to you?*
>
> He didn't say anything but he focused the camera on me. And then they chased him away . . . They searched me, they were looking for money but I didn't have any. Then one hit me with his rifle and said, 'Get away from here, go to that field.'

As we were walking along, we came to this house. A woman in camouflage uniform came out. She had a gun. A young man among us was wearing a camouflage shirt. She said, 'Where did you get that, Turk?' and then she told him to go into the house. What happened next, I don't really know. And then we went to the field and sat there. They kept molesting people, asking them for money. They beat people. They hit them on the head with their rifles. I couldn't watch this any more.

Enver was ordered by a Serb soldier to fetch water for the men as it was a hot day and most were begging for something to drink.

I kept getting water and I had to obey their orders. I did whatever they wanted me to ... One of them said: 'Let them have the water before we kill them ...'

PANORAMA: *The men who were sitting on the field, where were they being taken?*

They were being taken to this house one by one ... They were selecting people to take to the house, they didn't touch the wounded. They were taking certain people and saying, 'Don't worry, your turn will come. There's no need to be afraid. You're just going in for interrogation,' but nobody was coming out again.

PANORAMA: *Did you hear any noises from the house, any sounds of voices, any sounds of gunfire or anything?*

I could hear banging noises, nothing else ... Some rumbling. I didn't hear screaming. It sounded as if something was being hit.

PANORAMA: *What condition were the men in, who were waiting on the field, who were sitting down?*

They were exhausted. They didn't have any food. They were pale and terrified. They knew what was awaiting them – I did too. They knew they were going to be killed. They were praying to be simply killed. I heard people whispering that they were hoping to be killed without being made to suffer.

At another site, in the village of Kravica on the Bratunac–Konjevići road, 52-year-old Hakija Huseinović was herded into an agricultural warehouse. Inside the dark building the men were huddled together

rotection. The Serbs were firing randomly into the warehouse.
einović told *Panorama*:

> When it got dark, the shooting stopped. There was a lot of
> screaming, shouting, people were crying out for help in the
> warehouse. Many were wounded. As I lay down, the right-hand
> side of my body got soaked in blood. I couldn't stand it any
> longer, so I got up from the blood and pulled a dead body
> underneath me to lie on top of it. When dawn started breaking,
> [my neighbour] Zulfo Salilović got up to urinate and have a
> drink of water. I tugged at his coat and told him, 'Stay down,'
> and he said, 'I can't hold it any longer.' A machine-gun burst
> cut him in half and he fell down. I covered myself with two dead
> bodies and stayed underneath for twenty-four hours. During the
> day I heard someone calling 'Salko, Salko.' He repeated it about
> twenty times. [Then someone said] 'Fuck your Turkish mother.
> You're still alive.' There was a rifle shot. You couldn't hear the
> voice again. Afterwards, a truck and a mechanical shovel ap-
> peared. They started tearing down the side of the warehouse
> facing the road, then they started loading. They loaded until
> nightfall. The shovel came very close. I was thinking, 'This is
> the end for me. All that fear has been in vain,' but you have to
> keep hoping whilst you're still alive. And then I heard someone
> say, 'Park the shovel, wash the tarmac and cover the dead bodies
> with hay. It's enough for today.'

Later that night, Huseinović managed to escape, together with another
man.

The process was not one of random, indiscriminate violence. It was
orchestrated. In his dealings with Dutchbat, General Mladić had made
it clear that one of his priorities was the screening of the 'men of
fighting age' for 'war crimes'. Radovan Karadžić backed up this
demand, by careful omission, when he stated to the foreign press, 'Our
army is very responsible. People, civilians as well as UN personnel, are
completely safe and secure.' In other words, Muslim soldiers were fair
game. But making the careful distinction between innocent people,
civilians, men of fighting age, soldiers and war criminals was not a
problem which greatly troubled the Serb soldiers and their leaders.
Basically, all the men in the enclave were regarded as enemies and

legitimate targets, and a conscious and deliberate effort was made to kill them.

What Enver Husić had witnessed taking place inside the house along the road from Bratunac was part of a preliminary screening process. A sizeable group of men appear to have been identified at this stage, who, for whatever reason, were deemed to warrant further investigation. These were sent to Bratunac mainly during the Thursday afternoon and evening, where they joined the men from Potočari. Here the main screening process took place. One of the Muslims who survived the ordeal told Human Rights Watch:

> We ended up spending the night in the truck [which had taken them to Bratunac], 119 of us, crammed together. During the night, guards would come around with guns and shout. They were looking for certain people from certain places, especially from Kamenica, Žedenska and Glogova. Here I recognized Milan Gručić from Orahovica . . . We went to the same school for one year. I was a year younger.[9]

The screening to which the men were subjected was systematic, up to a point. In 1993, the Serbs compiled lists of Muslims whom they alleged committed war crimes against Serbs during the early stages of the war. The lists included places of birth because regional origin was deemed important in establishing possible affiliations to specific gangs or territorial defence units the Serbs suspected of having raided particular villages. Local Serbs assisted in identifying the men who, as in the above account, were sometimes classmates or even friends of their accusers. Despite shared histories, it was these local Serbs who tended to be the most motivated to hunt down their former neighbours, whom they blamed for all the hardship and terror they and their families had suffered in the war.

In the final analysis, however, these interrogations were not meant to distinguish the guilty from the innocent. Everyone was slated for execution, if for no other reason than that they had witnessed events the Serbs did not want advertised in detail to the rest of the world. The screening process seems largely to have existed to provide solace to the executioners: to sustain the delusion that they were engaged in a legitimate campaign to identify and eliminate the enemies of the Serb nation.

Paradoxically, the vast majority of Muslim men who were of political or military importance in the Srebrenica enclave successfully evaded capture. The Serbs did catch at least one big fish: Ibran Mustafić, the leader of the SDA (Party of Democratic Action) in Srebrenica and in third place on a Serb list of 'organizers of the crimes' perpetrated by the Srebrenica Muslims. Yet, as is so often the case in war, a person's importance, or the suspicion of importance, provided the best assurance of survival, and in April 1996 Mustafić was exchanged for an important Serb prisoner, Colonel Aleksa Krsmanović.[10] Some wounded men, whom the Serbs removed from two medical convoys, also survived, it seems, for the same reason. The Serbs were very suspicious of the wounded because they believed that suspected Muslim 'criminals' hid in their midst with affected injuries. For example, some fifty wounded Muslim men who had remained in Potočari with the Dutch until 17 July were all carefully filmed and photographed by the Serbs. Seven were subsequently identified as suspected war criminals and, with the other wounded, were taken to the hospital in Bratunac. Although a Dutch doctor saw them there, he was lured away at some point and the seven disappeared. Later that month the Red Cross found them in Batković prison. They were exchanged for captured Serbs.

During the night of Wednesday 12 July, the mass of the Muslims who had evaded capture and almost certain death moved west, towards the surroundings of Nova Kasaba. Under cover of darkness, many succeeded in crossing the road in between Nova Kasaba and Konjevići. Dr Ilijas Pilav crossed at about three o'clock in the morning. A few hundred metres from the road, he came to the Jadar river. As he followed the river north for a while, he noticed many drowned men. They had been simply too exhausted to make it across.

The men who did make it across were following in the wake of the surviving elements of the 28th Division of the Bosnian Army and the Srebrenica Presidency, who had already moved past the vicinity of Cerska and then paused for the day on the slopes of Mount Udrč. This territory had once been inhabited by Muslims. Now the troops and politicians moved through a wasteland of ghost towns. Early the next evening, 14 July, the 28th Division ran into what they estimated to be around 300 Bosnian Serb troops with anti-aircraft guns in the vicinity of Liplje, just south-west of Zvornik. After a two-hour fire-fight, the Muslims were able to break loose and continue their trek. They were now getting close to Bosnian government territory. By this time the men were exhausted beyond reason and their food supply had completely run out. Suljo Hasanović recalled:

> We came to Kriŝevići at 04.00. We slept in the forest that night and rested. We ate what we found: the roots of some plants. We knew that we were ten kilometres from our territory. We agreed that everybody who was in better shape and who had weapons, must cut the Četnik lines at Baljkovica.

Eventually, contact was established with the Bosnian troops on the other side of the Serb lines. In the afternoon of 15 July, a coordinated attempt was made to break through. The heroes of the hour were Naser Orić, who had been in charge of Srebrenica until April 1995 and who now led the troops from the Bosnian government side, and Ejub Golić, who commanded the Srebrenica soldiers from the other. The fighting lasted for over a day. The members of the Srebrenica Presidency remained behind the front line and waited anxiously. Ejub Golić was killed. Some men lost their nerve and committed suicide. None the less, the mass of the Bosnian group slowly started to trickle over the front lines. The Presidency reached safety in the early after-noon of Sunday 16 July.

But many more of the men from Srebrenica never even made it beyond Nova Kasaba. The Serbs had captured them in their hundreds over Wednesday night and throughout Thursday. Perhaps because the numbers were getting too large for transport to Bratunac, they were assembled in the football ground just north of Nova Kasaba.

On Thursday, Dutch soldiers spotted an estimated 1,000 men squat-ting on the football pitch. It was the largest group of prisoners they had seen while escorting convoys from Potočari. That same day, an American U-2 spy plane photographed some 600 people crowding the pitch, surrounded by what appeared to be guards. When the plane returned some days later, the football pitch was empty, but it noticed that a nearby field had changed in appearance: it showed signs of recent digging, and experts identified what they believed to be three mass graves. Tracks from heavy vehicles led to the field from the road. (When the photographs were discovered in August 1995, journalist David Rohde of the *Christian Science Monitor* evaded Serb patrols to visit the field. He reported finding recent digging and, in one place, 'what appeared to be a decomposing human leg protruding from the freshly turned dirt'.[11] In the vicinity of the mass graves he discovered identification papers and other documents, mentioning Srebrenica and other near-by localities, as well as Muslim prayer beads and empty ammunition boxes.)

On Thursday evening 13 July, some Dutch soldiers were forced by the Serbs to spend the night in Nova Kasaba 'for their own safety'. Between 02.30 and 03.30, they heard repeated small-arms fire to the north of the town, where the football pitch and the grave site were located. The next day, two Dutchbat soldiers saw 500 to 700 bodies along the road.

On Friday and Saturday, the Serbs were busy clearing the road, from Milići all the way to Bratunac, of any lingering evidence. Dutch soldiers witnessed many bodies being removed in an odd assortment of pick-up trucks, tractors with carts and vehicles with shovels. The personal belongings of the Muslim men, which had littered the road, were collected and burnt. A UN Commission report described the experience of a Dutch soldier who had been captured in the early stages of the Serb attack on Srebrenica:

> On Saturday 15 July, when he was being transferred from Simići to Bratunac, he passed a football ground near Nova Kasaba. On a section of the football pitch, he saw a row of the shoes and rucksacks of an estimated 100 men. Shortly afterwards he saw a tractor with a cart on which there were corpses. Approximately 500 metres further along he saw another row of the shoes and equipment of approximately twenty to forty people. Here he saw a tip-up truck carrying corpses on an excavator. Finally, he observed a body in the bend of the road.[12]

The only large group of men from Srebrenica who remained alive on Friday 14 July (in addition to the soldiers who fought their way out further north) were in Bratunac. Many of these had been arrested in Potočari. They had been kept in the Bratunac football stadium and in a local school. On Thursday evening 13 July these 'Potočari men' were joined by those who had been seized along the Bratunac–

Konjević road. Because of overcrowding, many of the new arrivals were kept overnight in trucks and buses. Interrogations, torture and selective executions took place throughout the night.

By Friday, Bratunac was emptied of Muslim men. The operation was well-organized and conducted by disciplined troops, whose reign of terror extended to playing mind-games with the prisoners. One survivor recalled:

> We stayed in the buses [in Bratunac] until 11.00 a.m. the next morning (July 14), when the policeman said that we would be transported to Kladanj. There were six buses and four trucks full of people. Later the convoy stopped to wait for the other vehicles to catch up, and a white UN transporter with caterpillar tracks showed up. For a second I thought we'd be saved, that we'd be exchanged [for Serb prisoners], but when I saw the Četniks saluting and talking to the four UN soldiers who turned out to be Četniks themselves, I realized it was all over.[13]

Probably with the same buses and trucks that had been used to deport their women and children on the previous days, the men were taken to a school complex in Karakaj near Zvornik.

> The Četniks took us out of the truck one by one; we had to keep our hands behind our necks and yell, 'Long live Serbia! Srebrenica is Serbian!'[14]

The men were taken to large classrooms. Others were crammed into a gymnasium. During the day and evening, individuals and small groups were taken away for interrogations, beatings and selective executions. The men were ordered to strip to the waist and take off their shoes. In the classroom, once darkness had set in, the same survivor recalls:

> [We] were ordered to run out into the corridor. We were running barefoot on a floor which was covered in blood. I saw about twenty corpses lying near the front door. They beat us while we climbed into the trucks with our hands tied behind our backs. I got into the truck when it was just half full. The Četniks kept on yelling to load more and more people into the truck until it was crammed full, and then they closed the back.

They ordered everyone to sit, but we couldn't because it was so tightly packed with people whose hands were tied behind their backs. The Četniks started to shoot at people in order to make us sit down.[15]

The terror was kept at a constant level. The objective – as emphasized by the forced running, the beating and the yelling – was to instill the execution process with a sense of inexorable movement and speed. No one, including the executioners, was given an opportunity to question the process. An awareness of the magnitude of the final horror that faced the Muslim men was thus dulled. The 17-year-old Nezad Avdić described his arrival at the site of his intended execution:

When the truck stopped, we immediately heard shooting outside . . . The Četniks told us to get out, five at a time. I was in the middle of the group, and the men in front didn't want to get out. They were terrified, they started pulling back. But we had no choice, and when it was my turn to get out with five others, I saw dead bodies everywhere. A Četnik said, 'Come on *Balije*,[16] find some space.' We stood in front of the Četniks with our backs turned to them. They ordered us to lie down, and as I threw myself on the ground, I heard gunfire. I was hit in my right arm and three bullets went through the right side of my torso. I don't recall whether or not I fell on the ground uncon-scious. But I remember being frightened, thinking I would soon be dead or another bullet would hit. I thought it would soon be all over. While lying there I heard others screaming and moaning . . . During one of the following executions I felt a sharp pain in my foot . . . The man next to me was moaning, and one of the Četniks ordered the others to check and see what bodies were still warm. 'Put a bullet through all the heads, even if they're cold.' Another Četnik replied, 'Fuck their mothers! They're all dead!' Only one Četnik came over to the pile and shot the man next to me, and I felt stones hitting the upper part of my right arm. He continued his job until he was done. Later I heard a truck leave. I didn't know what to do. First I thought I should call them to shoot me and finish me off, but then I decided to look up. I saw someone moving about ten metres away from me and asked, 'Friend, are you alive?'[17]

Avdić and his new-found companion managed to escape the field of death. After a number of days they made it to Bosnian territory. At another execution site, Mevludin Orić and Hurem Suljić also survived and escaped. They were joined three days later by another man, Smail Hodzić, who appears to have been the last of five survivors from the Karakaj massacre.[18]

Another execution site for the men held in the Zvornik area was near the state farm outside the village of Pilica. There are no known survivors.[19] But a participant in the killing has come forward, the 25-year-old Dražen Erdemović. He gave an interview to the French daily *Le Figaro* on 8 March 1996 and, subsequently, testified to the War Crimes Tribunal in The Hague. Erdemović had a varied, though for the Bosnian war not exceptional, background. A Croat from Tuzla, with a Serb wife, he had served with the JNA, Bosnian Army and Bosnian Croat Army. But when trying to escape the war in Bosnia, he got stuck in Serb-held territory in November 1993. Erdemović claimed not to have had a choice but to join the Bosnian Serb Army and ended up with a special unit, the eighty-men-strong 10th Sabotage Detachment, commanded by Lieutenant Milorad Pelević. Its task was described by Erdemović as 'sabotage behind enemy lines' and 'the elimination of troublesome people'. The unit came under the direct command of the military headquarters of the Bosnian Serb Army.

Erdemović's unit arrived in the town of Srebrenica on 11 July and was subsequently sent to a military barracks in Zvornik. There, on the morning of 16 July, the eight-man squad of which he was a part received the order to go to the state farm of Pilica. They were given no information about the task awaiting them. Armed with Kalashnikov automatic rifles and an M84 machine gun, they were told on arrival, by the squad commander, Branko Gojković, that they would have to execute Muslims from Srebrenica. The soldiers lined up waiting for their victims to arrive. There was a lot of drinking.

Soon after, a bus arrived with what Erdemović believed to be some sixty men of military age:

> Two members of the military police of the Drina Corps made ten people get off the bus and led them to about twenty metres from the line which we formed. We were given the order to fire.

The next group of ten men taken off the bus saw what had happened to the first group:

> They begged us 'Don't shoot us! Our families in Austria will send you money.' One of my comrades yelled at the Muslims, 'Whoever possesses Deutschmarks will be spared.' But Branko said, 'Don't bother, they have taken everything from them in Zvornik.'

More and more busloads arrived. To speed things up, Gojković decided to use the machine gun. But it was not as accurate as the rifles. Many of the victims did not die instantly but were only wounded. They begged their executioners to finish them off. According to Erdemović, one of the squad members, Stanko Stovanović, obliged them. Later, Stovanović claimed to have used 700 bullets.

In all, the squad dispatched fifteen to twenty busloads of men. Erdemović estimated that some 1,200 men were killed in five and a half hours, of which he 'only' shot seventy. The terrified and horrified bus drivers were also made to kill at least one Muslim, 'so that they would never be tempted to confess later'. After they finished, Erdemović's unit received the order to execute another 500 or so men who were held in the cultural centre in Pilica. This they refused.

Why did Erdemović participate in such a heinous crime? He testified in The Hague that he believed he had no choice. When he tried to save the life of one Muslim with whom he had engaged in conversation, commander Gojković responded that no Muslim witnesses should survive and Erdemović could join the other line if he wanted. It requires no exceptional men to commit exceptional crimes.

We will never know how many men were killed exactly. The accounts of survivors, along with statements by Dutch soldiers, Bosnian women and Serbs, are difficult to evaluate. Individual witnesses may exaggerate, or underestimate, the numbers of dead.[20] They may misunderstand or misrepresent the circumstances under which people died. Every perspective can only be partial. However, the pattern and the vastness of the tragedy cannot be disputed.

Of the large group of Muslim men who anticipated their fate and who tried to break out of the enclave, several thousand were captured alive. Many of these men were seen by Dutchbat soldiers, Muslim women and children and photographed by American spy planes and satellites. A Serb commander named Janković boasted that he had captured 6,000 Bosnian Army soldiers.[21] Erdemović estimated that he had participated in the execution of some 1,200 men. One thing that is clear is that subsequent official Bosnian Serb claims that most of the men had been killed in combat cannot be true. Although there is evidence of fighting during the night and morning of the break-out attempt, the convoys transporting the women and children from Potočari witnessed none. All convoys passed through the very same area where the fighting is supposed to have taken place. What they saw was dead bodies and prisoners.[22] The Petrović video, which was taken around 16.30 on 13 July, shows relaxed Bosnian Serb soldiers, whistling tunes, smoking cigarettes and listening to music on the radio, while armoured vehicles are firing bursts of heavy machine-gun fire into the woodlands adjoining the road and Muslim men are still surrendering.

There is no evidence that the substantial number of prisoners who were seen alive along the road from Bratunac to Kladanj were ever released or are still being detained. According to Red Cross files, over 1,700 men were last seen alive in Potočari by their families. Virtually all of these men are still missing. By August 1996, only a few hundred Muslim prisoners had been traced, and the Red Cross believes there are no more camps with Srebrenica survivors.[23]

The best indication of the number of people who were killed in combat and executed by the Serbs is provided by the Red Cross. At the time of writing, the Red Cross list of the missing from Srebrenica contains 6,546 names, virtually all men. The total number of registered missing for the war in Bosnia as a whole, including those from Srebrenica, is some 11,000 Muslims, Serbs and Croats. Unless one suspects that the screening processes developed by the Red Cross over the course of a century are insufficient and that the organization is the victim of a massive fraud, this seems likely to be the approximate death toll. It may decrease a little because some men who hid in the forests of eastern Bosnia may not have notified the Red Cross after reaching safety. A year after the event, however, it is unlikely that any *more* men will emerge from the forests.

Under international humanitarian law, the summary execution of prisoners of war and/or civilians constitutes a war crime. What is more, in that their actions in and around Srebrenica violated the 'elementary dictates of humanity', the Serbs were also guilty of crimes against humanity. There was a 'systematic process of victimization' of the Muslim population that included, as article 5 of the Statute of the Tribunal in The Hague states, 'murder, extermination, . . . deportation, imprisonment, torture, rape, persecutions on political, racial and religious grounds and other inhumane acts'. But beyond even that, the Serbs' actions constituted an act of genocide. The Srebrenica massacre was 'committed with intent to destroy, in whole or in part, a national, ethnical, racial or religious group, as such'.[24] Two questions resound. First, and simply, why did the Serbs attack the safe area of Srebrenica and systematically kill so many of its male inhabitants? Second, why did the international community not protect the safe area and prevent its fall? The rest of this book will attempt to provide an answer.

NOTES

1. That the Serbs were waiting in the area seems to be supported by the fact that, compared to the other OPs in the north, east and west of the enclave, OP Mike witnessed more Serb military activity close by. On Thursday 6 July, already, the crew was forced by Serb fire to withdraw towards Jaglići and set up a new OP closer to the town.

2. Human Rights Watch/Helsinki, 'The fall of Srebrenica', p. 30.

3. Human Rights Watch/Helsinki, 'The fall of Srebrenica', p. 31.

4. Human Rights Watch/Helsinki, 'The fall of Srebrenica', pp. 32–33.

5. Human Rights Watch/Helsinki, 'The fall of Srebrenica', p. 32.

6. Van Laerhoven, *Srebrenica*, p. 122.

7. Van Laerhoven, *Srebrenica*, p. 127.

8. Anthony Lloyd, 'Srebrenica's exiles tell grimly familiar stories of murder', *The Times*, 15 July 1995.

9. Human Rights Watch/Helsinki, 'The fall of Srebrenica', p. 39.

10. BSA Colonel Krsmanović was arrested by Bosnian government police, together with General Djordje Djukić, on 30 January 1996 and transferred to the International Criminal Tribunal in The Hague. Unwilling to cooperate as witness, he was returned to the custody of the Bosnian police on 29 March.

11. David Rohde, 'Evidence indicates Bosnia massacre', *Christian Science Monitor*, 18 August 1995.

12. 'Final periodic report on the situation of human rights in the territory of the former Yugoslavia submitted by Mr Tadeusz Mazowiecki, special rapporteur of the Commission on Human Rights, pursuant to Paragraph 42 of Commission Resolution 1995/89', United Nations Economic and Social Council, E/CN.4/1996/9, 22 August 1995.

13. Human Rights Watch/Helsinki, 'The fall of Srebrenica', p. 39.

14. Human Rights Watch/Helsinki, 'The fall of Srebrenica', p. 40.

15. Human Rights Watch/Helsinki, 'The fall of Srebrenica', pp. 40–41.

16. *Balije* is a derogatory term used for Muslims by Serbs.

17. Human Rights Watch/Helsinki, 'The fall of Srebrenica', p. 45. The two men were to have been killed at a site now known to human rights investigators as Sahanici One.

18. Emma Daly of the *Independent* (4 April 1996) visited the gymnasium where two of the survivors were allegedly held: 'Inside the hall, debris supporting the witnesses' stories was everywhere: spent rifle shells, odd shoes, spatters of what looked like blood, discarded blindfolds, even a swathe of the same pink material from which the blindfolds had been roughly cut. The scene stank.'

19. There is the curious story of one Resid Halilović who was reportedly found badly bleeding by some local Serbs in Loznica in the afternoon of 15 July. He was taken to hospital, but subsequently disappeared, according to Robert Block of the *Independent* (25 July 1995), who tried to trace him. A Resad Halilović appeared on the same Serb list as the aforementioned Ibran Mustafić under the heading 'organizers and leaders of armed activities'. Possibly he was a survivor from the massacre at Pilica.

20. Since police forces find it extremely difficult to estimate correctly the number of people in demonstrations, how much more difficult must it be for an individual in the middle of a crowd to know how many people surround him with any precision?

21. *Handelingen Tweede Kamer, 1995–1996*, 22 181, No. 134, 30 November 1995, p. 27.

22. The claims of Muslim men who successfully escaped that they were continuously shelled and attacked can therefore also not be entirely true.

23. By November 1995, the Red Cross had only found some 193 Muslim prisoners from Srebrenica in Serb hands. In April 1996, 211 men were released from Sljivovica in rump-Yugoslavia, while thirteen were still detained as suspected war criminals. On 1 May 1996, the Belgrade authorities released another five Muslims.

24. Art. II of the 1948 Convention on the Prevention and Punishment of the Crime of Genocide.

Part Two

Srebrenica, Safe Area

CHAPTER FOUR

The First Srebrenica Crisis:
March–April 1993

On 16 January 1991, six months before the Yugoslav war of dissolution began, Serbian President Slobodan Milošević had lunch with ambassadors of the European Community countries. He told them that if Yugoslavia were allowed to break up, Serbia would seek to carve out a new Serbian state. He made it clear that this state would not be restricted to the 'administrative entity' of Serbia proper, but would be 'the fatherland of all Serbs'. Milošević warned, 'the Serbs who want to return to the Serbian fatherland have the right to do so and the Serbian nation will enforce that right.' Milošević said he was prepared to let Slovenia go. Macedonia was still under discussion. But he wanted to be absolutely clear about the Serb-inhabited parts of Croatia and about Montenegro and Bosnia-Herzegovina: they would remain part of the Yugoslav federation. He issued an explicit warning to the ambassadors:

> The position which I have sketched for you now, is the ultimate compromise Serbia is willing to accept. If this is not attainable peacefully, one forces Serbia to use the tools of power which we possess, but they do not.

The Serbian plan for creating a new state with new borders boded ill for the small town of Srebrenica in the eastern part of the Republic of Bosnia and Herzegovina, close to the border with Serbia. For, according to Milošević's vision, eastern Bosnia was to become part of this new, 'greater', Serbia.

Already in September 1991, local Serb leaders had announced the creation of 'Serbian Autonomous Regions' within Bosnia. This act put them on a collision course with the Muslim-dominated Bosnian government, which was trying to keep the Republic together. At the same time, military preparations for war were under way. The 90,000 troops of the Yugoslav People's Army (JNA) that were deployed in Bosnia started conducting massive exercises. Officially, these manoeuvres were meant to deter violence by paramilitary and local defence forces from all sides: Serb, Croat and Muslim. In reality, the exercises were covert preparations for war – a war that the JNA planned to enter on the side of the Serbs in Bosnia.

The Yugoslav People's Army was, in fact, fast becoming a Serbian army. The dissolution of Yugoslavia presented it with a fundamental problem neatly summarized by the Federal Defence Minister, General Veljko Kadijević: an army cannot exist and operate 'without a clearly defined state'.[1] With Yugoslavia falling apart, what new state could the army serve? Even before the conflict in former Yugoslavia erupted in 1991, the officer corps had been dominated by Serbs. Close to two thirds of officers before 1990 and almost all senior officers claimed this ethnic origin. Obviously, these men were already looking towards Serbia. The choice was made easier by the fact that Slobodan Miloše-vić's Serbia identified itself officially with the continued existence of the federal Yugoslavia. (Serbia and Montenegro proclaimed the Federal Republic of Yugoslavia on 27 April 1992.) The JNA's enemies were those bent on destroying the old Socialist Federative Republic of Yugoslavia: the Slovenian and Croatian nationalists and Bosnian Muslim 'fundamentalists'. The logical objective seemed therefore the creation of a new Yugoslavia in which all those supporting the federal ideal could live. In practice, with the defection of non-Serb officers and rising Serb nationalism, this meant the creation of a Greater Serbia in which non-Serbs would no longer pose a threat to the unity of the state.

The Autumn 1991 exercises were a cover for the redistribution of the weapons confiscated by the JNA to the Serb Territorial Defence Forces. They also established the army's presence in key strategic locations. Early in 1992 the Serbs were poised for action. Their moment came after a referendum in Bosnia – boycotted by the Serbs – overwhelmingly supported independence, leading President Alija Izetbegović to declare Bosnia-Herzegovina an independent and sover-eign state on 6 March 1992.

Following incidents in late February and early March, the Serb campaign in Bosnia began on 27 March 1992. In the space of little more than two weeks the cities commanding the roads into Bosnia from Serbia and eastern Croatia were taken by Serb forces. Foča, Čajniče, Višegrad, Zvornik, Bijeljina, Bosanski Brod and Derventa fell in quick succession. Kupres, a town controlling the main road through the vital heights in western and central Bosnia, was also captured. With these major towns in their hands, the roads connecting them were opened up, as well as those leading to Sarajevo, Pale (the seat of the Bosnian Serb government) and Banja Luka, which was the major Serb stronghold in western Bosnia. By May, at the end of a six-week campaign, Serb forces had occupied some 60 (and ultimately 70) per cent of the territory of Bosnia-Herzegovina – even though Serbs only constituted 31 per cent of the population.

Nearly everyone was taken by surprise by the suddenness and the magnitude of the operation. Alarmed UNHCR officials noted that 'almost overnight the republic broke apart'. The number of displaced persons was huge. By 12 April, UNHCR roughly estimated that 10,000 people had fled from Zvornik, 5,000 from Čajniče and Goražde, 5,000 from Foča, 2,000 from Bosanski Brod and 5,000 from Kupres. At the same time, there was fighting in Sarajevo. Despite the clearly distinguishable pattern, most people did not realize the extent of the complicity of the JNA and the careful planning that had gone on. On the face of it, the breakdown in order was the result of the activities of Serbian paramilitaries. Even President Izetbegović initially believed so, and on 1 or 2 April he asked the army for assistance in protecting Bijeljina. The JNA gladly provided it: by late afternoon of 3 April, the army had occupied the whole town. Order, as Izetbegović hoped, was not restored.

The attacks on the border towns followed a standard pattern. A ring of roadblocks, generally manned by JNA troops, would appear around a town. Serb inhabitants then received a warning to evacuate. Once they had gone, heavy artillery and mortars opened fire at the Muslim and Croat inhabitants. (At Zvornik, army batteries were conveniently located across the border, in Serbia proper.) Such bombardments lasted from several hours to several days. The already terrorized population, who were either trying to flee or hiding in their cellars, would then come face to face with their greatest enemy: the paramilitaries.

Once a town was judged to have been softened up sufficiently by the JNA's artillery, paramilitary groups would move in. The objective of such groups as Arkan's Tigers, Vojislav Šešelj's Četniks and Mirko Jović's White Eagles was to 'ethnically cleanse' the town. The fall of Višegrad offered a typical example:

> On 13 April 1992, the city of Višegrad was occupied by the Užice Corps. This group consisted of JNA soldiers, reservists, Užice territorial defence forces, and White Eagles . . . The corps then broadcast a message instructing the residents to return to Višegrad and assuring their safety . . . The JNA then blocked all roads leading out of Višegrad with help from the White Eagles and Užice Corps. Soldiers at the roadblocks would take away Muslims, whose names appeared on a master list. Between 18 and 25 May, the Užice Corps left Višegrad, leaving it to fall under the control of the White Eagles, Četnik gangs and Šešelj's forces . . . the killing and torturing of Muslims began. Residents could not leave the city without permission. Many Serbs were seen throwing bound Muslims into the [Drina] river to drown them. In early June, many girls were taken to the Hotel Vilina Vlas, interrogated, and raped. Some of the females were not returned.[2]

The paramilitaries generally performed the most gruesome and difficult parts of these operations. They were specially suited to the job. Most of the large paramilitary organizations were allied to or integrated into Serbian political parties. Šešelj also led the Serbian Radical Party and Jović had his Serbian People's Renewal. Arkan openly acknowledged the organizational and financial support of the Serbian Orthodox Church and himself led the Serbian Unity Party. Many paramilitaries had a criminal background. Arkan, whose real name is Željko Ražnatović, was active as a criminal in Western Europe long before the war broke out. He has a number of international arrest warrants outstanding for, among other things, armed robbery, murder and car theft. For people like Arkan, the war offered great opportunities for financial gain through plunder and extortion.

The paramilitaries thus possessed the nationalist conviction and material motive to commit murder in the service of the nation. Yet, by themselves these factors do not explain the persistent and widespread participation of the paramilitaries in the war, nor the scale of their success. None of the militias was directly linked to the Serbian government party of President Milošević, nor to the dominant Serb party in Bosnia, the SDS of Radovan Karadžić. None the less, it is clear that they operated under instructions. Not only did the paramilitaries boast of their contacts with the Serbian government, but even Serbian government officials themselves, hurt by the attention the militias were attracting at home, stressed the important role official structures played in their support. Already regarding the war in Croatia in 1991, Colonel-General Života Avramović, the Yugoslav deputy defence minister, stated:

> the contribution made by small-sized [paramilitary] units cannot be compared to the operational-strategic achievement of the JNA's units . . . In reality, without the JNA, not a single 'guard' would be able to defend the Serbs successfully from the Ustase knife and even less to hold on to the front dividing [our] people from the enemy.[3]

Indeed, the logistical requirements of the militias simply dictated that they had to be supplied by the Yugoslav state and army. Where else could they get their stocks of weapons and ammunition consistently replenished? Moreover, according to two not widely advertised laws of July and December 1991, the framework was created to include the paramilitaries in the JNA and accord them regular status with all related benefits.

Yet, to the outside world the connection was not so obvious. The absence of overt links with Milošević's government made it possible for him to deny responsibility for the crimes the paramilitaries committed. Thus the image was reinforced that the cleansing was a by-product of aberrant behaviour by 'irregulars', who were operating outside government control. The conflict was depicted by Serb propagandists as one caused by age-old nationalist hatreds and its excesses restricted to deviant individuals.

Though many people *were* 'indiscriminately' killed, tortured, beaten and threatened, the process was anything but random. The first objective was to force the Muslim populations to flee their home towns and create an ethnically pure Serb territory. A certain amount of immediate, 'demonstrative atrocity' was therefore deemed necessary. The more random and indiscriminate the terror and violence, the easier this goal would be achieved. The second objective was to minimize possible future Muslim resistance. To the Yugoslav military, steeped in the Titoist tradition of territorial defence and people's war, every man was a potential fighter. Thus, men of military age were singled out for particularly brutal treatment. In Višegrad, one observer witnessed a paramilitary gunman announcing, '"The women and children will be left alone . . ." As for the Muslim men, he ran his finger across his throat.'[4]

Among the able-bodied men, the ones with the bleakest future were those associated with positions of public authority and respect. In Bratunac 'the local Muslim cleric reportedly was tortured in front of the townfolk, who had been rounded up in the soccer stadium, was ordered to make the sign of the cross, had beer forced down his throat, and then was executed'.[5]

The process of tracking down these individuals was a careful and calculated one. As in Višegrad, lists with the prominent Muslims were drawn up prior to attack. In many places, a parallel local government administration had also been set up some time before. A so-called *Krizni Štab*, or 'Crisis Headquarters', comprised of local Serb political leaders and police, would be ready to take over power and organize the removal of the Muslim and Croat local élites. The people on the lists were rounded up and either summarily executed or sent to detention centres. Since their number tended to be substantial, local police stations usually could not cope. Other, larger facilities were therefore used. For example, the detention centres of Omarska, Keraterm and Manjača were, respectively, an iron-ore mine and processing plant, a ceramics factory and a former army barracks. Here the inmates were subjected to a harsh regime of malnutrition, beatings and interrogations, which in many cases ended in executions.[6] To assist the process, local Serbs who were known to the victims were often involved in both the process of arresting and interrogating individuals. 'The main objective of the concentration camps, especially Omarska but also Keraterm,' a UN report concluded,

> seems to have been to eliminate the non-Serbian leadership. Political leaders, officials from the courts and administration, academics and other intellectuals, religious leaders, key business people and artists – the backbone of the Muslim and Croatian communities – were removed, apparently with the intention

that the removal be permanent. Similarly, law enforcement and military personnel were targeted for destruction.[7]

Two of the defining characteristics of the Serbian war in Bosnia-Herzegovina were that it was highly organized and that ethnic cleansing was part of a deliberate strategy.

By the end of May 1992 the frontline stabilized and remained essentially unchanged until the summer of 1995. The Serbs controlled western Bosnia, except for an enclave around Bihać. Most of eastern Bosnia was also in their hands. Their initial offensive, centring on the strategic road network, had only failed in taking Goražde. The strategically less important area surrounding Žepa, Cerska and Srebrenica had been bypassed. But it would only be a matter of time before the Serbs would get around to dealing with the enclaves. After the opening campaign of the war in March–May 1992, the Serbs took their time consolidating their gains. They concentrated on ethnically cleansing their newly won territory. The summer and autumn of 1992 saw massive population movements. By the end of the year, two million people, nearly half the population of Bosnia, were refugees. The majority were Muslims. They were herded towards Bosnian-government-held territory in central Bosnia and towards the enclaves.

Although their ethnic-cleansing campaign in eastern Bosnia ran smoothly on the whole, it did not go the Serbs' way everywhere. The Muslims of Srebrenica had been issued an ultimatum by Serb militias in neighbouring Bratunac to hand in their weapons by 10.00 on 18 April 1992 or else to face attack. The Muslims knew from refugees what had taken place in Zvornik and Bratunac, and many took cover in the densely forested hills surrounding the town. Determined to avoid the grim fate of their fellow Muslims, they held on to the few weapons they had. After the expiry of the ultimatum, Arkan's Tigers and other militias entered Srebrenica and started looting and killing elderly Muslims who had stayed behind. But in the hills surrounding the town, small groups of Muslims were preparing to counter-attack the Serbs. One such group was commanded by Naser Orić, a 25-year-old policeman, whose strong, compact physique presented an intimidating figure, later reinforced by his mujahedin-style short, cropped hair and beard.

Orić was born in March 1967 in Potočari. In the 1980s he moved to Belgrade, where he joined the special military police. He excelled and, in spite of being a Bosnian Muslim, was promoted to become a bodyguard to Serbian President Slobodan Milošević. But with the outbreak of war in Yugoslavia he resigned and returned to defend his native region against the Yugoslav People's Army.

On 20 April, two days after the occupation of Srebrenica, Orić and a group of men descended from the hills and attacked the Serbs, killing several. That day, Orić was elected as commander of the territorial defence. He had proved to be a brave and skilled leader and was the natural choice to lead Srebrenica in the forthcoming battles against the Serbs.

In early May, the Serbs stepped up their attempts to establish control over the Srebrenica area. The JNA shelled the Muslim villages, and the militias tried to enter them with infantry. These 'mopping up' operations were carried out by a coalition of paramilitaries from Serbia and a militia comprised of Serbs from Srebrenica and Bratunac. The leader of these local Serbs was Goran Zekić, a judge and a local SDS politician. On 8 May, after two days of gun battles, Zekić was ambushed and killed. His death proved to be the start of a mass exodus of Serbs from Srebrenica to Bratunac. The Muslims had won control of the town, but the Serbs exacted a terrible revenge for their defeat: in the Bratunac football stadium they executed scores of male Muslim prisoners.

As soon as control had been established in Srebrenica, Orić and his commanders began to launch attacks against Serb hamlets and villages to the south and east. Srebrenica provided just about the only case in Bosnia where the much-vaunted Yugoslav territorial defence system was successfully applied by the Bosnians. The main aim of the raids from Srebrenica was to obtain weapons and ammunition. Suljo Hasanović, who commanded a 'battalion' of Muslim soldiers until he was wounded, recalled,

> We were not ready for war. We had to attack to get arms and ammunition. We attacked south because the Serbs were weak there. They did not think that we would dare to attack towards Serbia. Another important factor was food. We had to obtain food. We had many refugees from Zvornik, Bratunac, Rogatica and Han Pijesak. Srebrenica itself is an industrial town. The area

west of Srebrenica is mountainous. South is where the good agricultural lands are. Besides, we simply wanted to liberate as much as possible of the Srebrenica *opština*.

Between May 1992 and January 1993 forces from Srebrenica attacked and destroyed scores of Serb villages. The attacks outraged the Serbs. A great deal of the animosity towards the men of Srebrenica stems from this period. The Serbs put a lot of effort into collecting evidence of war crimes committed by Muslims in such villages as Brežani, Zalazje, Ratkovići, Fakovići and Glogova. Evidence indicated that Serbs had been tortured and mutilated and others were burned alive when their houses were torched. Over 1,300 people were reputedly killed during this period.

By the end of December 1992, Orić and his men controlled 95 per cent of the Srebrenica *opština* and half of the Bratunac *opština*. Though they had conquered and ethnically cleansed a vast area, Orić's forces were not as strong as they seemed, for they were short on food and ammunition and still surrounded by Serbs. The civilian and military leaders in the enclave, who had joined to form a war council in July, knew that Srebrenica could not survive a concerted Serbian offensive if no link was established with other Muslim-held territories in eastern and central Bosnia.

In September 1992, forces from Srebrenica had linked up with Žepa, a Muslim-controlled enclave to the south. To the north, in the Cerska enclave, an equally desperate battle was being fought by Muslim forces under the command of the prescient Ferid Hodžić. As commander of the Bosnian territorial defence in Kamenica, Hodžić had tried to warn his fellow Muslims before the war began to organize themselves, rather than hand in their weapons to the Yugoslav People's Army. Over the summer, Hodžić's forces pushed north, towards Bosnian government-held central Bosnia, and south, towards Srebrenica. In October, his forces attempted to meet up with Bosnian forces from Teocak, commanded by Captain Hajro Mešić. As Hodžić recalls:

> In October, we tried to link up with Teocak. We were hoping to meet Hajro's men in Nezuk, west of Zvornik. But we lacked the weapons and the ammunition and we never broke through. Hajro died on 30 October in a last attempt to make a link.

Srebrenica, Cerska and Žepa therefore remained cut off from the outside world, and the humanitarian situation inside the enclaves deteriorated quickly. It was not until the end of November 1992 that the UN was able to get a convoy with relief supplies into Srebrenica. It was the first convoy to arrive in over six months of war. A fortnight after the convoy arrived, Muslim forces from Srebrenica launched a major raid towards the Drina river. In the early morning of 14 December several hundred Muslim fighters descended on the village of Bjelovac and, according to Serb sources, killed some fifty Serbs.

A complex game was taking shape in which the Bosnian government was trying to exploit the desperate situation in the enclaves. A UNHCR official later explained to Lord Owen why he thought Orić had attacked so soon after the arrival of the convoy:

> In Eastern Bosnia the situation is complicated. The Muslim pockets there were used by the Sarajevo government in November as pressure points on the international community for firmer action. The longer that aid convoys were unable to reach them, the greater the pressure on the [UN] mandate. When convoys did succeed, calls for firmer action were unwarranted. Two weeks after the first successful delivery Muslims launched an offensive towards Bratunac. Thus the integrity of UNHCR and UNPROFOR was undermined, further convoys were impossible, and the pressure for firmer action resumed.

Without doubt the politicians in Sarajevo used the enclaves in eastern Bosnia as pressure points on the international community. However, the attack, which was followed by others in December and January, also had a military rationale. Orić (and Hodzić did the same from the Cerska enclave) created a diversion which supported a major Bosnian Army 2nd Corps offensive to cut off the Posavina corridor connecting Serbia with both Serb-held western Bosnia and the Krajina in Croatia. Miralem Tursunović participated in the operation:

> The aim was to break the Serb corridor and create one for ourselves between Tuzla and Croatia. We advanced quickly and met Croat forces from Orasje at Krepčić. We controlled the corridor for fifteen days. But Serbian forces with tanks counter-attacked from the direction of Bijeljina and we had to withdraw

to Boce and Palanka. On 31 December 1992 and 1 January 1993 we cut the corridor for the second time but after forty-eight hours we were again forced to retreat.

If the corridor remained cut, the Serb areas to the west would very quickly run out of vital fuel and ammunition supplies, all of which had to be brought in from Serbia.

Orić and Hodžić wreaked as much havoc as they could. Their success was amplified because the Serbs had been forced to thin their lines around the enclaves to reopen the corridor. This created an opportunity to connect Cerska and Srebrenica. To do so, Orić and Hodžić would have to take Glogova and Kravica, two Serb-held villages located on the main road between the two enclaves. Glogova was attacked and destroyed on 24 December by forces from Srebrenica. Kravica, however, was more strongly defended by 400 Serb soldiers. In the early morning of 7 January, Orthodox Christmas, a large Muslim force launched a surprise attack on Kravica from the direction of Konjević Polje. The fighting was ferocious, but at the end of the day the Muslims drove out the Serbs. Over 100 Serb soldiers and civilians were reputedly killed.

With Kravica in Muslim hands, Srebrenica and Cerska were finally linked. There was now one large enclave stretching from Kamenica in the north to Žepa in the south. All of this land was envisaged as part of the Muslim-majority Tuzla province under the Vance–Owen plan. But the Muslim success was short-lived. By January 1993, the Serbs had reopened their corridor and Serb tanks and artillery were being directed south. On 8 February the Serbs attacked Kamenica in the north of the Cerska enclave. That day Lord Owen received a short report from UNHCR warning, 'The Serb intention is to achieve a military victory in this region and to open a corridor to Tuzla in order to facilitate the departure of those civilians who want to leave.' The Serbs had begun what they saw as their final push for a Muslim-free eastern Bosnia. The Muslims themselves remained isolated and were no match for the much better-equipped Serbs. Without outside help of some kind, they were doomed.

As a result of the continued Serbian offensive against the east Bosnian enclaves, the humanitarian situation inside them was deteriorating rapidly. A UNHCR report of 19 February 1993 described the situation in Srebrenica:

> There is no food such as we know it. They have not had real food for months. They are surviving on the chaff from wheat and roots from trees. Every day people are dying of hunger and exhaustion. The medical situation could not be more critical. People who are wounded are taken to the hospital where they die from simple injuries because of the lack of medical supplies. They have problems of epidemic proportion with scabies and lice.

Since road convoys were unable to reach the enclaves, the new US President, Bill Clinton, suggested air drops to relieve the situation. Between March and June 1993, some 1,900 tonnes of food and medicine were dropped around Srebrenica. The weakness of the air-drop operation, however, in the view of one UN official, was that the Serbs 'might interpret the operation as a signal that Washington wants to stay out of Bosnia, leaving them to carry on their ethnic-cleansing programme'.[8]

This seems to have been borne out because the beginning of the air-drop campaign coincided with a rapid advance by the Serbs against the Muslim-held village of Cerska. On 1 March, in their first operation, US planes dropped food on Cerska. But the Serbs had advanced further than realized and the pallets landed behind Serb lines. Cerska itself fell that same day.

Thousands of refugees from Cerska fled to Mount Udrč, the highest mountain in the area, where they waited in vain for three days and nights to be evacuated by the UN. Though the UN was trying hard to organize an evacuation, Serb generals refused to allow any international presence in the area and coldly warned that the offensive would continue in the direction of Srebrenica.

The fall of Cerska and reports that Serb soldiers were killing civilians stirred the UN Security Council in New York into action. On 3 March, the Council requested the UN Secretary-General, Boutros-Ghali, to 'take immediate steps to increase UNPROFOR's presence in eastern Bosnia'. The next day, the UNPROFOR commander for Bosnia-Herzegovina, French General Philippe Morillon, announced he would go to Cerska. He said he had received permission from the Bosnian Serbs and that he and Mladić had provisionally agreed to create a corridor for civilians from Cerska, Žepa and Srebrenica to reach government-held central Bosnia.

Morillon, a wiry 57-year-old with penetrating, somewhat melancholic eyes, had been in Bosnia since the beginning of the war. Independent-minded and wayward, in the early 1960s he had supported the coup attempt by the French military against President de Gaulle – which did not seem to have impeded his career. Morillon believed he knew the Serbs well (he had spent two years in Yugoslavia as a French military representative) and was convinced he could deal with them.

The French general arrived in nearby Konjević Polje the next evening, where he met Orić and Hodžić. Both men had fought hard to slow down the Serb advance, but the battle for Cerska had been lost and they told Morillon that Konjević Polje would be the next target of the Serb advance. Morillon felt that Orić and Hodžić were exaggerating the gravity of the situation. As he had promised, the next morning Morillon went to Cerska to check out the reports that atrocities had taken place there. When he returned to Sarajevo, he told the press, 'I have not smelled death.' Morillon explained that although people had no doubt been killed during the battle for Cerska, he had 'found no traces of massacre after the battle'.[9]

Morillon had promised Orić and Hodžić that there would be a corridor for the civilians, but as soon as he returned to Sarajevo, the Serbs added a new condition. Before there could be a corridor, they now demanded, some 10,000 Serbs from Tuzla should be given safe passage to Serb-held territory. The Tuzla authorities were furious, as they believed that the Serb demand was merely a delaying tactic. Eventually, a few hundred Serbs indicated that they wanted to leave Tuzla and were allowed to do so. But in the meantime, the Serb offensive had continued unabated. In fact, as soon as Morillon had left Konjević Polje, the Serbs stepped up their attacks. While negotiations over a corridor dragged on, the Serbs began to bombard Konjević Polje, forcing more and more Muslim refugees southwards into the Srebrenica pocket. It was clear that the Serbs would not stop until they had seized full control of the Bratunac–Zvornik–Vlasenica road.

On 8 March, while Mladić's tanks and howitzers were shelling Konjević Polje, Mladić himself was discussing a ceasefire and a corridor with Morillon and the commander of the Bosnian Army, General

Sefer Halilović. Mladić offered a free passage for women, children and old people. As for the men, he implied that they would be at the mercy of his army. Halilović, in desperation, withdrew from the talks and publicly ordered his troops in central Bosnia to launch an offensive towards the enclaves, 'to prevent the massacre of innocent people'.[10] The offensive had no chance of success. Colonel Andjelko Makar, a Croat, popular with his subordinates, who had left the JNA to become the Chief of Operations in the Bosnian 2nd Corps, thought Halilović's order was unrealistic:

> We were ordered to attack towards Srebrenica. But Serb tanks and artillery had opened up the corridor and they were now trying to take Gradačac and push us back to Majevica. All our forces were engaged in defending Gradačac, Brčko, Olovo and Tesanj. We were so heavily engaged defensively that whomever ordered us to attack towards Srebrenica did not understand that we simply could not.

Morillon soon learned that the Serbs had continued their offensive after he had left Konjević Polje. He had ordered a contingent of British UN troops, commanded by Major Alan Abrams, to stay in Konjević Polje to oversee the evacuation of wounded people from Cerska. In his war memoirs, Morillon recorded:

> At that moment I learn that the Serbs have not halted their offensive and that after Cerska, they have bombarded Konjević Polje, chasing the inhabitants under the horrified eyes of the blue helmets present. Abrams saw, with rage in his heart, women and children die. His own vehicles were hit, some destroyed. He had to withdraw, with the inhabitants having fled into the mountains while carrying their wounded . . . [11]

Alarming reports about the situation in Srebrenica were also coming in from Simon Mardel, a British doctor of the World Health Organization, who had reached the town after a five-hour walk from Konjević Polje. Mardel reported that people were dying at the rate of twenty to thirty a day. He estimated that 170 wounded needed to be evacuated as soon as possible and that up to 18,000 women and children also wanted to be evacuated. Contacting his government in Paris, Morillon told them that he feared that the Serb intention was to 'cleanse' all of eastern Bosnia and that another Vukovar was in the making. If this were to happen, the peace talks chaired by Vance and Owen would inevitably collapse. The French government shared his assessment. Morillon felt that if he could stabilize the situation on the ground, he could save both Srebrenica and the peace process. He decided to go to Srebrenica and turn the world's attention to the plight of the isolated enclave.

On 11 March, Morillon received permission from the Serbs – who, the general believed, were 'grateful for his objective reporting' on Cerska – to cross the Serb front line at Bratunac with a convoy of three vehicles and to go to Srebrenica.[12] But the Serbs had blown up the bridge on the main road between Bratunac and Srebrenica, forcing Morillon and his party to take a narrow snow-covered forest path, which the Serbs knew had been mined. Slowly, the small convoy progressed towards Srebrenica. It was already getting dark when they encountered a small group of Muslim men defending the front line. As they were talking, the truck carrying medical supplies suddenly hit a mine and toppled over. The Belgian drivers were rescued and the group quickly moved on to Srebrenica. Morillon was received by members of the war council that same evening. Knowing what had happened in Konjević Polje, the leaders of Srebrenica deeply mistrusted Morillon. But they also knew that he was their only hope. Srebrenica was being attacked from all sides. Refugees from Konjević Polje were sleeping in the streets. The situation was hopeless.

The next morning Morillon held a meeting with Naser Orić, a few deputy military commanders and the civilian leaders. Morillon told them he would try to arrange a ceasefire and negotiate access for humanitarian aid convoys. The general urged them to refrain from any provocations. He suggested that Srebrenica could become a demilitarized zone. After the meeting the Srebrenica war council held a private meeting in which troubling questions were raised. Who was going to protect Srebrenica if it was to be demilitarized? How could they be sure that the Serbs would demilitarize too? One of the people present at the meeting later recalled:

> Morillon discussed demilitarization with Orić and the war council. We had to ask [the Bosnian government in] Sarajevo for a decision on such a matter. Sarajevo supported it because there was nothing else.

In the afternoon, Morillon told the leaders that he would leave the handful of UN military observers and peacekeepers who accompanied him behind, while he himself would depart from the enclave to negotiate a ceasefire.

During Morillon's presence in Srebrenica the Serbs had not fired a single shell on the town itself. With the UN general in their midst, the people of Srebrenica had begun to feel more secure. They feared that if he left, the shelling would start again, as had happened in Konjević Polje. When Morillon climbed into his vehicle that afternoon, he was surrounded by a crowd of women and children who refused to let him leave. Orić had received a coded radio message from Srebrenica's exiled mayor, Murat Efendić, who was now in Sarajevo. Efendić told Orić, 'Whatever happens, prevent Morillon from leaving Srebrenica until he provides security for the people there. Do it in a civilized way. Use women and children.'[13] The women needed little prompting. They were mobilized by Fatima Huseinović, the president of the Women's League, which had been founded in May 1992 to enable the women to do their part in Srebrenica's fight for survival.

> I was on my way to the hospital when I ran into my neighbour. He told me, 'Morillon wants to leave. You are president of the Women's League. Can't you do something to keep Morillon here?' I decided to organize the women. I went to the post office, where women and children were looking at Morillon and I thought, 'We must keep him.' I found a woman who lived near the post office and said to her, 'Let's go from house to house, assemble the women and children and tell everybody to go to the post office.' I made signs and posters. That is how we blocked Morillon's car.

Morillon was surrounded by a sea of women and children. Some women lay in front of his vehicle. He could not move. Smoking one cigarette after the other, he negotiated with the women for hours until he finally accepted that he had been taken hostage. He decided to make the best of it and walked to the balcony of the post office (PTT), where he told the women: 'You are now under the protection of the UN forces . . . I will never abandon you.' Seemingly resigned to his fate, Morillon went back into the post office to get some sleep.

But in spite of his fresh commitment to the people of Srebrenica, he still believed his job lay elsewhere. Morillon decided to sneak out of the enclave in the early hours of the next morning. He left the town on foot at 02.00 to meet a transport vehicle at a prearranged location. But he had been spotted and waited in vain for hours. The vehicle, presumably held up by the Srebrenica authorities, never arrived, and Morillon walked back to the PTT building in the early morning.

Later that day Morillon signalled his staff at UNPROFOR's Bosnia-Herzegovina headquarters in Kiseljak that he considered himself a hostage of the Bosnians in the PTT building. He believed the Bosnians would not allow him to leave until three conditions were met: 1) a halt to the Serb offensive; 2) maximum humanitarian aid; and 3) the entry of UN military observers (UNMOs) into the area, particularly along the Drina river, where much of the artillery firing on the enclave was located. Morillon requested that UNPROFOR do the following:

> a) Recommend that the maximum pressure be applied at the highest level towards Belgrade and Bosnian-Serb authorities to stop the Serb offensive.
> b) Accelerate the humanitarian effort by sending an aid convoy waiting in Zvornik immediately and to study the feasibility of opening an air corridor into Srebrenica pocket to evacuate up to 200 wounded as soon as possible.

The UN was hardly in a position to exert pressure on the Bosnian Serbs. On the contrary, as soon as it was clear that Morillon had remained in the enclave, the Bosnian Serbs began to demand his departure as a precondition to lifting the blockade. In a meeting with two UN representatives from the Kiseljak headquarters, Dr Lukić, the 'prime minister' from the self-styled Bosnian Serb Republic, claimed that the Muslims were using Morillon's presence in Srebrenica for 'blackmailing purposes'. This was something, Lukić added, that the Serbs did 'not appreciate for both military and political reasons'. He claimed that the Serb position on the passage of humanitarian convoys – 'free passage allowed after all contents have been checked' – had remained the same, but that Morillon should first leave the enclave. After the general's departure, humanitarian aid and the evacuation of wounded civilians would be allowed and there would be 'freedom of movement for people seeking refuge from Srebrenica'. Fed up with the Serbs' intransigence, Morillon eventually ordered UNPROFOR to begin air evacuation without their permission. But the operation had to be aborted when the French and British helicopters carrying it out came under fire.

Within the UN organization many people felt very uncomfortable with Morillon's approach. Instead of leading the UNPROFOR operation in Bosnia, some felt, the commanding officer had placed the lives of himself and his party in danger. Now it was up to his staff in Sarajevo and Kiseljak to bail him out. In New York, Morillon's superiors in the UN Secretariat were angry that he had not consulted them before going into the enclave. They feared that they were losing control and that Morillon was pushing the UN into the role of a 'safe area' protector: a responsibility that the UN Secretariat was anxious to avoid.

On 13 March, the Srebrenica war council allowed Morillon to leave the enclave, but he decided to stay. The general told his staff, 'My intentions are to remain here myself as long as an agreement for the opening of a helicopter air corridor has not been achieved.' He added, 'I wish negotiations to be started for the deployment of one company of Canbat [Canadian battalion] 2 to this area.' On 15 March, the International Conference on the former Yugoslavia in Geneva (ICFY) received an update about the situation:

> General Morillon at 10 p.m. last night confirmed his intention to remain within the Srebrenica pocket until the situation improved. He advised that tension with the local population was decreasing and relations with UNPROFOR were improving. He reported approximately 1,500 refugees living in the streets around the PTT building. There were many wounded lying on stretchers and it was understood many more wounded were lying in the outlying villages. He assessed that the Serb intention was to reduce the enclave village by village. Heavy fighting, mortar and artillery fire was continuing on villages a few kilometres from the town. There was a successful drop of aid by six aircraft on the night of 12/13 March.

In the afternoon of 15 March, Morillon again set out to meet Serb commanders to negotiate a ceasefire. He also wanted to show the

Serbs, whose media were insisting that Morillon was a prisoner in Srebrenica, that he was 'absolutely free' in his movements. Again refugees tried to prevent him from leaving, but this time the war council cooperated. On the destroyed bridge west of Bratunac, the UN general met General Manojlo Milovanović, the chief of staff of the Bosnian Serb Army. Milovanović agreed to an immediate halt of the Serb offensive, as soon as the attacks by Muslim forces against Vlasenica stopped and General Halilović publicly retracted his order to attack. On contacting the Bosnian government, UNPROFOR quickly received a promise from Vice-President Ejup Ganić to make such a statement. Morillon then suggested to Milovanović that some kind of UN protected area might be created around Srebrenica, Skelani, Cerska and Bratunac. Milovanović merely promised to pass the idea on to Mladić. Milovanović again insisted that before any aid convoy would be allowed to enter Srebrenica, Morillon would have to leave the town. Morillon refused this last condition and returned to Srebrenica.

While Morillon was negotiating with the Serbs, the last Muslim resistance in Konjević Polje was broken. UN military monitors predicted that the Serbs could take Srebrenica within three to four days. They reported that Muslim forces were lacking in weapons and ammunition and were unable to block the simultaneous Serb advances from the north, east and south. The monitors also reported that artillery and aircraft from Serbia proper were supporting Bosnian Serb operations and that in all probability Serbia had allowed the Bosnian Serb Army to deploy tanks from within Serbian territory to attack Srebrenica from the south.

There was little Morillon could now do. By their actions, it was clear that the Serbs had effectively rejected the idea of a protected area before it had even been properly entertained and that they aimed to conquer the territory. On 18 March Morillon was approached by Naser Orić, who was in daily contact with General Halilović and had recently spoken to Ejup Ganić, and asked Morillon whether Srebrenica could become an open city. The conversation with Orić led Morillon to come up with a proposal to demilitarize the town. He informed his staff in Kiseljak:

You probably know that Ganić asked for this town to be an

open town, placed under UNPROFOR protection. My intention is that except for some Civpol [civilian police] designated by the Presidency in order to maintain the peace in town, all men who wish to stay here must give their weapons to my command post here in Srebrenica. Those who want to continue to fight must go to the hills or preferably try to cross the front line. This is my proposal, I want you to be aware of that and to inform Zagreb and New York.

Orić agreed with Morillon's proposal. But while a UN officer in Srebrenica reported that Orić had ordered his forces to hold their fire and to cease all offensive actions, the Serbs continued attacking. The Muslims were losing territory in the south-west corner of the pocket.

For several days now Morillon had negotiated in vain to get convoys into Srebrenica, where people were dying of hunger. On 18 March, Morillon gave up trying to obtain permission and ordered a Danish relief convoy blocked at Zvornik to proceed towards Srebrenica. It was turned back by the Serbs. After another failed attempt the next day, Morillon travelled up to Zvornik to negotiate its passage in person with Captain Pandorević, the local Bosnian Serb Army commander. Pandorević consulted Mladić and agreed to let the convoy go to Srebrenica, but only without its military escort. The convoy was forced to drive down the Bosnian bank of the river Drina, where the road was very bad. The vehicles could only move slowly. But at approximately 22.00 on 19 March, the first convoy since November 1992 was led into Srebrenica by Morillon himself. Hans Ulens, a Belgian sanitation expert working for Médécins sans Frontières, was in one of the trucks that reached Srebrenica that evening:

We were waiting for permission to get out of the cabin. People were all over the trucks, pressing 100 DM bills against the windows. It was strange and I wondered what they wanted for that money. I first thought it was food. But it was not the food they were interested in. It was cigarettes, for God's sake! Everybody wanted to buy cigarettes! The price for one packet of cigarettes was 100 DM. I had never realized how important cigarettes can be for people in a war situation.

It was night and the temperature had dropped to −5 degrees Celsius.

The streets were covered in a thick layer of snow. As soon as the convoy had been unloaded, nearly 700 women, children and elderly scrambled on to the trucks. Most of these people were refugees from Cerska and Konjević Polje and possessed nothing but the clothes they wore. They were desperate to be evacuated. But the convoy did not leave until the next morning, and the refugees were forced to stand on the trucks all night. When the convoy arrived in Tuzla the next evening, several women and children had died of asphyxiation, exhaustion and exposure. To those waiting in Tuzla, the arrival of the convoy from Srebrenica was a shocking experience. People began to realize the extent of the tragedy that was unfolding in the *Podrinje*, the land under the Drina. The refugees were hungry, cold and dirty and were surrounded by a sickening stench. Their wounds had been neglected and amputations had to be performed immediately as gangrene was eating away at people's bodies.

Meanwhile, Morillon had left Srebrenica and was working hard to arrange a ceasefire. On 26 March, he and other senior UN personnel met Milošević and Mladić in Belgrade. Morillon announced that he had obtained an agreement from Mladić to observe a Bosnia-wide ceasefire, which was to begin at noon on 28 March. Mladić himself announced that the UN could bring relief supplies to Srebrenica and evacuate the sick and the wounded and all others who wished to leave, provided they left their weapons behind. Morillon had also asked Mladić to allow a company of Canadians to be stationed in Srebrenica. Mladić promised to consider the matter and give an answer in the next two days.

In spite of the announcement, Serb Captain Pandorević in Zvornik continued to block a convoy destined for Srebrenica. Only when the agreement had come into force two days later did he allow it to continue on to Srebrenica. The local authorities and the international staff inside the enclave had identified some 750 people who urgently needed to be evacuated. But in the early morning of 29 March, the trucks were stormed by thousands of women. They were in an absolute state of panic and were desperate to get on one of the nineteen trucks. Some mothers threw their babies aboard before trying to climb aboard themselves. Old women were thrown off by younger and stronger women. Instead of the intended 750 people, more than 2,400 climbed aboard. The convoy left later that morning and met Mladić at the repaired Bratunac bridge. Mladić suggested to Laurens Jolles, the UNHCR officer overseeing the evacuation, that instead of nineteen trucks, the UN should come in with '300 trucks daily' to move everyone out more quickly.

The Bosnian government was getting worried and opposed further evacuations. It wanted Srebrenica to become a safe haven, protected by UN forces. If the evacuations from Srebrenica continued at this rate, there would soon be no substantial civilian population left. Without civilians whose lives were directly under threat, the pressure on the United Nations to deploy peacekeepers in Srebrenica would subside. On 30 March, the sixth UN convoy in ten days was on its way from Srebrenica to Tuzla, carrying another 2,500 refugees. The Bosnian military were furious and summoned the major international organizations in Tuzla to the headquarters of the 2nd Corps for an emergency meeting with General Karić, the deputy commander of the Bosnian Army. While summoning them over the telephone, Abdulah Bašić, the 2nd Corps' liaison officer and an influential member of Izetbegović's Party for Democratic Action, vented his anger and threatened the international officials: 'The convoy is not allowed to come in. We are ready to sacrifice these people.' During the meeting the Bosnian Army delegation explained that a mass evacuation from Srebrenica was 'not in the interest of Bosnians and contradictory to their military goal'. Although the convoy blocked outside Tuzla was eventually allowed in, the issue of a mass evacuation was not resolved.

As Mladić was relaxing his grip on Srebrenica to allow the UN to take more people out, the Bosnian government continued to block further evacuations. Mladić decided to step up the pressure. On 1 April, he announced that from now on only empty trucks could travel to Srebrenica.

In response to Mladić's announcement a letter was sent to the Security Council by the highly regarded UN High Commissioner for Refugees, Mrs Sadako Ogata. In her letter, Ogata explained that even if Mladić were to reverse his decision, the efforts UNHCR were making would be totally inadequate. She argued that there were only two options if the lives of those trapped in Srebrenica were to be saved:

1) To immediately enhance the international presence, includ-

ing that of UNPROFOR, in order to turn the enclave into an area protected by the UN, and inject assistance on a scale much greater than permitted at present. Such an option would require the strongest political pressure from the international community on the Serbian side, or:

2) A large-scale evacuation of the endangered population, which would require the cooperation of all parties concerned, in particular the Bosnian authorities, as well as massive international support to UNHCR to ensure that it was conducted in a manner which did not endanger the lives of those it was meant to save.

The United Nations faced a terrible dilemma: should they evacuate the people and stand accused of facilitating ethnic cleansing, or should they continue to try, and in all likelihood fail, to deliver aid to the enclave? The organization was not alone in its predicament. On 4 April, the UNHCR special envoy to former Yugoslavia, José Maria Mendiluce, was told by President Izetbegović that 'your dilemma is our dilemma'. After some hesitation, Izetbegović agreed to an evacuation of the wounded civilians, elderly over sixty and women with small children. The Bosnian President himself was in two minds, while his government was split. Vice-President Ganić, epitomizing the hard-liners in the Bosnian government, rejected·evacuations. But Bosnian Foreign Minister Haris Silajdžić was inclined to accept that Srebrenica was lost and that it was now a matter of saving not the territory but the people of Srebrenica. Soon after Izetbegović had given his half-hearted consent, Silajdžić informed Mendiluce that he wanted the UN to 'consider a mass evacuation of civilians out of Srebrenica'. But Silajdžić was in a minority, and no more mass evacuations took place.

At a subsequent press conference, Mendiluce pointed out that UNHCR's primary role was 'to save as many people as we can'. He announced that the UN planned to evacuate 15,000 refugees from Srebrenica. In response to charges of UN complicity to ethnic cleansing, Mendiluce explained that the UN, in line with the options presented by Mrs Ogata, was pursuing a 'two-track approach'. While aiming to evacuate those people who wished to leave, it was also seeking to bring food supplies to the town and deploy peacekeepers in the enclave.

The UN's two-track approach could only work if, despite all the tensions, the truce held. But the Serbs, believing that the Bosnian government had succeeded in blocking further evacuations and that the situation was not likely to be quickly reversed, had become impatient and decided to take Srebrenica. On 5 April the Serbs renewed their attack. The town was subjected to further shelling and the hospital was hit. The water supply was cut off when advancing Serbs captured the water purification plant at Zeleni Jadar, seven kilometres south of Srebrenica. Although Muslim forces recaptured the site the next day, they could not restore the town's water supply as the Serbs had mined the plant.

Fearing that the ceasefire he had negotiated was collapsing and that a tragedy might yet befall Srebrenica, Morillon set off again for the town on 6 April. He ordered 120 Canadian UN troops in Tuzla to follow him. But Mladić had never responded to Morillon's earlier request for access for the Canadians and now refused to give it. The general himself was stopped at Sokolac, fifty kilometres outside Sarajevo, where after seven hours of negotiations he was told to leave three vehicles behind. Continuing with two vehicles, he got as far as Zvornik. There he was surrounded by a crowd of furious Serb widows who blocked his passage and painted the words 'Morillon Hitler' on the UN vehicles.[14] After many hours, it was General Milovanović who, openly defying the UN-declared no-fly zone, arrived by helicopter and extricated Morillon from the crowd. Milovanović's helicopter then flew Morillon to the front-line at Caparde, from where he had to walk through no man's land to get to Tuzla. Morillon arrived in Tuzla devastated: he had failed to honour his personal obligation to the people of Srebrenica. The UN's humiliation was plain for everyone to see. To rub salt into the wound, the first convoy in the planned mass evacuation had been forced to return to Tuzla empty by the Srebrenica war council.

Around Srebrenica, the fighting was getting fiercer by the day. Strong Serb attacks were followed by desperate pinprick counter-attacks by the Muslims. On 12 April, the situation in Srebrenica itself reached a new low, when two short intense artillery bombardments killed fifty-six people, including children, and seriously wounded seventy-three others. Hans Ulens, the MSF employee, wrote a letter to his head office in Belgium, describing the day's events. He was in the hospital when the wounded arrived. It only had one operating theatre:

> Within twenty minutes over seventy wounded arrive, among them many hopeless cases ... In a few moments a painful decision has to be made. Cases with little chance of survival or who need protracted operations are refused in order to offer the others a greater chance of survival; a logical decision under these circumstances, but a dramatic one for the mothers, fathers and family members who are told that their child, brother or sister has to wait. For many of them it will be too late.

By 13 April, the fall of Srebrenica was imminent. The Bosnian Serb Army bit off another chunk from the enclave and took Skenderovići, just east of Srebrenica. The next day, mayor Hajrudin Avdić called a meeting with the international staff still present in the enclave. Avdić, who was later replaced by one of Orić's men, told them that the war council wanted to capitulate if the wounded soldiers were evacuated. Since the message was too sensitive to be relayed to Sarajevo by radio, the only UNHCR official left in Srebrenica, the Frenchman Jean Claude Amiot, offered to take out the message to the UNHCR office in Belgrade. The next day Amiot left with a small convoy that the Serbs assumed contained all of the remaining international staff. As soon as it had left, the Serbs launched a massive attack on the Muslim lines.

While this was happening, the Russian and American envoys to the former Yugoslavia, Vitaly Churkin and Reginald Bartholomew, were in Belgrade, trying to convince Milošević and Karadžić to order a halt to the offensive. The two Serbian leaders were adamant that there was no intention to take Srebrenica. Milošević and Karadžić were well aware that Srebrenica was ready to surrender: it had even been announced on Belgrade radio. But they also knew that the Security Council was on the verge of adopting not only a resolution declaring Srebrenica a safe area but also another one imposing further financial sanctions against the Serbs. On 16 April, Churkin signalled from Belgrade that Milošević and, to a lesser extent, Karadžić had come to understand that it might not be in the interests of the Serbs to take Srebrenica. Milošević began to send out messages that indicated that he had himself decided against the seizure of Srebrenica, but that it was far from certain that Mladić could be stopped. In a telephone conversation with Lord Owen, Milošević said he was worried that the capture of the town would be accompanied by a 'bloodbath', as the Bosnian Serbs wanted revenge for the massacres of 1992 and early 1993 by the Muslims.[15] Subsequently, Milošević called UNPRO-FOR commander Swedish Lieutenant-General Lars-Erik Wahlgren and asked him 'to deploy military monitoring teams in and around Srebrenica' as soon as possible. Milošević told Wahlgren that Karadžić agreed with this. Though it was still unclear whether Mladić also agreed, Wahlgren ordered the Canadian company in Tuzla to prepare for departure to Srebrenica the following morning.

Mladić turned out not to agree, yet. While Milošević was busy constructing his own alibi, Mladić's forces broke through Muslim lines east of Srebrenica and advanced to within two kilometres of the town. From the high points of Pribićevac and Banja Crni Guber, the Serbs had a clear view of the town centre and were preparing to enter it. In the north-east, they broke through at Zalazje, while in the south they had pushed the Muslims out of Zeleni Jadar. In Srebrenica, people heard the shooting coming closer and closer and felt their chances of survival diminishing by the minute. An eyewitness who lived in the eastern part of Srebrenica offered the following account:

> Our house was located in the east of town on the road to Skelani. We were sitting in the basement and shells were exploding every five seconds. I could no longer sit still and just wait there, so I went upstairs to see what was going on. I went on to the balcony but immediately a machine-gun salvo hit the wall next to me. I went back to the basement. We could hear the shooting come closer and we thought we were going to be killed. Then suddenly I heard outgoing shells – a different sound. Either the Serbs had entered, or it was us! I went back up again and looked through the window. I saw more than a hundred men running up the hill towards the Serbs and I heard shouts: 'Naser, Naser!' Later I heard that Naser Orić and two groups of 150 men had pushed back the Serbs 500 metres that day. I also spoke with the artillery man who had fired the shells. He told me they had kept fifty shells for a critical moment. The artillery piece was located on a hill just out of town. When he saw that the Serbs

had taken our lines at Zalazje, he had fired twenty shells and the Serbs had withdrawn. During the whole battle we were listening to the radio. Two hours after Naser pushed back the Serbs, there was an announcement that Srebrenica had been declared a safe area. We all jumped into the air and fell into each other's arms, crying and laughing at the same time. We had been saved.

The radio report had been accurate. Shortly before midnight, New York time, the Security Council adopted Resolution 819, declaring 'Srebrenica and its surroundings' a safe area.

NOTES

1. Quoted in James Gow, 'The Role of the Yugoslav People's Army in the Yugoslav War of Dissolution', paper for the International Commission for the Balkans, Carnegie Endowment Aspen Institute, Berlin, 1996.
2. 'Final report of the Commission of Experts established pursuant to Security Council Resolution 780 (1992)', UN Security Council s/1994/674, 27 May 1994, Annex III.A, 'Special forces', paras 543 and 544.
3. Interview in *Narodna armija* (Belgrade), 12 March 1992, quoted in Paul Williams and Norman Cigar, *A Prima Facie Case for the Indictment of Slobodan Milošević* (London: Alliance to Defend Bosnia-Herzegovina, 1996), p. 39.
4. Blaine Harden, 'Serb forces overwhelm key town', *Washington Post*, 15 April 1993.
5. Quoted in Norman Cigar, *Genocide in Bosnia: The Policy of 'Ethnic Cleansing'* (College Station, Texas: Texas A&M University Press, 1995), p. 59, from a US Department of State, 'Submission of Information to the United Nations Security Council' of October 1992.
6. Sima Drljača, the secret police chief in Prijedor (and later the deputy minister of the interior of the Republika Srpska) said in an April 1993 interview with a Serb local newspaper that, 'In the collection centres "Omarska", "Keraterm" and "Trnopolje" more than 6,000 informative talks were held. Of this number 1,503 Muslims and Croats were sent to the camp "Manjača" on the basis of solid documentation of active participation in the fighting against the Army of the Republika Srpska, and also participation in genocide against the Serbian people. Instead of

letting them get their deserved punishment, the powerful men of the world expressing disdain forced us to release them all from Manjača.' 'Final report of the United Nations Commission of Experts established pursuant to Security Council Resolution 780 (1992)', para. 170.

7. 'Final report of the United Nations Commission of Experts established pursuant to Security Council Resolution 780 (1992)', para. 175.

8. Patrick Bishop and Peter Almond, 'US food aid "fell to the Serbs",' *Daily Telegraph*, 2 March 1993.

9. Michela Wrong and Louise Branson, 'General finds no atrocities, but refugees die by the dozen', *Sunday Times*, 7 March 1993.

10. Robert Mauthner, 'Bosnian push "to prevent massacre"', *Financial Times*, 9 March 1993.

11. Général Morillon, *Croire et oser: Chronique de Sarajevo* (Paris: Grasset, 1993), p. 166.

12. Morillon, *Croire et oser*, p. 165.

13. Laura Silber and Allan Little, *The Death of Yugoslavia*, second edn (London: Penguin and BBC Books, 1996), p. 267.

14. Reuters, 8 April 1993.

15. David Owen, *Balkan Odyssey* (London: Gollancz, 1995), p. 135.

CHAPTER FIVE

'Mission Impossible':
Designing a Safe-Area Policy

The idea of creating safe areas for the Muslim population in Bosnia was first floated in the winter of 1992 by Cornelio Sommaruga, the President of the International Committee of the Red Cross in Geneva. Sommaruga proposed to set up 'protected zones' based on the agreement of all parties to the conflict in Bosnia. The concept of a protected zone, safe area, safe haven, secure zone, or whatever one called it, had an inherent appeal. It seemed to offer a viable solution to the enormous humanitarian tragedy that had developed in the Muslim enclaves of Bosnia in 1992. Putting such a concept into practice, however, presented the international community with an insoluble problem. While the Red Cross supported it, very few other international bodies or countries favoured the idea. The UN, UNHCR, the International Conference on the Former Yugoslavia, the United States and the main troop contributors to UNPROFOR – Britain, France and Spain – all summarily rejected Sommaruga's suggestion. The proposal was supported only by a few smaller countries, who would not carry the burden of making the safe areas work. None the less, the idea resurfaced in spring 1993, when Srebrenica's fall appeared imminent. At this point, some of the countries that had opposed the idea in 1992 seemed overnight to have changed their view: they now supported the creation of safe areas. But they were as reluctant as ever to provide the means with which to make the areas actually safe.

A safe-haven concept had been applied successfully in northern Iraq to protect the Kurds in the aftermath of the 1991 Gulf War. The success in Iraq, however, had been dependent on a number of conditions that did not apply in Bosnia. First, a victorious coalition had just crushingly defeated the Iraqi army in Kuwait. The guarantors of the safe haven thus did not need to be seen as impartial, nor did they require the consent of the Iraqi government. Second, the safe haven covered a relatively large and contiguous piece of land that bordered on allied Turkey. Forces could thus easily be deployed and withdrawn. Third, the relatively open terrain allowed for effective air cover of the haven.

It was at a meeting with senior diplomats in Geneva in late October 1992 that Sommaruga first made his proposal for the establishment of 'protected zones' in Bosnia. Though Sommaruga's 'protected zones' were based on the prior consent of the three parties to the Bosnian conflict, his proposal was taken up in a different format by the Austrian Foreign Minister, Alois Mock. Mock began to support the idea of protected zones but left out the 'consent' aspect which Sommaruga deemed crucial. The Austrian foreign minister was well placed to rally support for the idea as Austria was on the UN Security Council. In New York, Austria quietly began to advocate the establishment of some form of safe areas. Austria obtained support from a number of members of the non-aligned movement, such as Venezuela and Morocco. The response to the Mock–Sommaruga proposal by the major powers on the Council was cool, but the Council did agree that the matter deserved to be looked at more closely. In resolution 787 of 16 November the Council 'invited' the UN Secretary-General, Boutros Boutros-Ghali, and the UN High Commissioner for Refugees, Mrs Sadako Ogata, to 'study the possibility of and the requirements for the promotion of safe areas for humanitarian purposes'.

Almost immediately after he had launched the idea, Sommaruga was warned about the risks involved in establishing protected zones by Lord Owen and Cyrus Vance, the co-chairmen of the International Conference on the Former Yugoslavia. For the protected zones to work, they would need the consent of both the Bosnian Serbs and the Bosnian government, and both parties would have to agree to demilitarize the zones. Vance and Owen doubted that this could be achieved in practice. Moreover, by declaring some areas safe, others would effectively be declared unsafe. This would facilitate rather than hamper ethnic cleansing. The Serbs would shunt Muslims into the 'safe' areas, while the Muslims themselves would seek refuge from the 'unsafe' areas.

The Security Council's permanent members were equally sceptical.

Resolution 787 called upon 'all parties' in Bosnia 'to end the blockade of Sarajevo and other towns and to demilitarize them, with heavy weapons under international supervision'. The insistence on all-party agreement and demilitarization indicated that key member states, like the United States, Britain and France, were not enthusiastic about the idea of formally declared safe havens, whose boundaries, they feared, would quickly turn into front lines. Franco-German-British talks on 27 November revealed that these three countries favoured instead the 'natural development' of 'zones of safety' or 'relief points' around already existing UN deployments, such as the French contingent in Bihać.

Unable to make further progress in New York and with Austria's term on the Security Council coming to an end, Mock decided to go public and give the idea a final push. In an interview with an Austrian newspaper on 3 December, he argued that *Sicherheitszonen*, or 'security zones', should be created around Sarajevo, Bihać, Tuzla, Goražde and Travnik. The job of protecting these zones, Mock said, would require perhaps 40,000 UN soldiers – far fewer than the 100,000 soldiers quoted by Western military sources as the minimum for a successful military intervention. Mock admitted that there was, as yet, little support for the setting up of his secure zones. The French were cautious, the British remained aloof and the Germans were unable to commit themselves for historical reasons. But he was not entirely without hope. The Austrian minister explained his intention to travel, with two European colleagues, to Washington and New York to seek backing from the outgoing US President George Bush and UN Secretary-General Boutros-Ghali, whose support, he felt, would override European scepticism.

The outgoing Bush administration responded negatively to Mock's proposal. The Defense Secretary, Dick Cheney, and the Chairman of the Joint Chiefs of Staff, General Colin Powell, opposed the idea because it would require a large reinforcement of the UN troops on the ground and significantly increase the level of risk faced by these troops. In addition, they believed safe areas would give the seal of approval to ethnic cleansing. Most crucially, there was general agreement within the Bush administration that the US could not promote the idea of safe areas while refusing to contribute troops to protect them.

Still, as stated, Austria was not entirely isolated. Some of Mock's strongest supporters were in the Netherlands, where a small number of influential people had for some time publicly advocated the idea of safe havens. Fatefully, one of these was Joris Voorhoeve, who later became Minister of Defence and, as such, was the person politically responsible for the presence of Dutch troops in Srebrenica in 1995. In an interview in the Dutch newspaper *Trouw* on 17 November 1992, Voorhoeve said:

> It is not my intention to argue for ending this war with military means – in that case one would have to occupy the whole of Bosnia. I just think that with 50,000 to 100,000 well-trained and well-armed troops protected areas for the civilians have to be created to end the slaughter.[1]

In a televised debate with Voorhoeve, General Arie van der Vlis, the Dutch chief of defence staff, warned that the soldiers protecting the safe areas would end up taking sides. Voorhoeve retorted that, indeed, the soldiers would take sides 'in favour of the threatened civilian population'.[2] Although Voorhoeve 'feared that what he saw as desirable, would not happen', he continued to advocate his idea. Yet, if the United States, France and Britain dismissed safe areas as an 'unreal exercise', who was going to establish and protect them? Which countries with troops on the ground would be willing to abandon the UN's impartiality and risk a war with the Serbs?

Despite international suspicion, Voorhoeve's idea found a receptive domestic audience and it was taken up by the government. At the end of November 1992, the Netherlands began to solicit international support for establishing safe havens. Within NATO, the Dutch suggested that a new UN mandate be given to the troops in Bosnia and that UNPROFOR be reinforced. A few days later, at an EC European Political Cooperation meeting on Yugoslavia, the Dutch repeated the proposal: safe havens protected by a strengthened UNPROFOR under an expanded UN mandate. They found little support for their ideas. The allies were unwilling to provide additional military resources and repeated their concern that safe havens would suck them into a long-drawn-out war with the Serbs. The Dutch had been rebuffed.

Yet soon the Alliance was forced to readdress the issue. On 11

December, Manfred Woerner, the NATO Secretary-General, received a letter from Boutros-Ghali who, following up on Resolution 787, requested UN access to NATO contingency plans on safe havens. Such plans did not exist. Although the NATO ambassadors, with the exception of the Dutch, remained unenthusiastic about the whole idea, they felt bound to take the UN's request seriously, and the decision was made for NATO to start contingency planning for safe havens.

The United Nations High Commission for Refugees had in the meantime finished its own study of the safe-area concept. It came to the same conclusions as Vance and Owen. 'Clearly delineated' safe areas, protected by UN forces, should only be a last option. As High Commissioner, Mrs Ogata pointed out to politicians that both the Croats and Serbs had made it clear to her that they would regard the boundary of secure zones as the front line. The Muslims were unenthusiastic, because they feared it would freeze the situation on the ground. Unless safe areas were part of a military interventionist strategy, it was unclear how they could contribute to an overall solution to the conflict.

On 19 December Cyrus Vance spoke before the Security Council and condemned the idea of formal safe areas as a recipe for further ethnic cleansing. For a while, it seemed that the idea was dead and buried. Attention in late 1992 shifted to the negotiations over the Vance–Owen Peace Plan, which was officially presented to the Bosnian parties on 2 January 1993. In this period, the Bosnian government also launched a number of offensives which, for the first time since the beginning of the war, appeared to achieve some military success. Under these circumstances, advocating the establishment of safe areas did not make much sense. It was not until March 1993, when the world's attention shifted towards the embattled town of Srebrenica, that the idea was resurrected.

On 16 April 1993, the Security Council adopted Resolution 819, which declared Srebrenica a safe area. The resolution was dangerously inconsistent. In the six hours of consultations prior to its adoption, a broad consensus had formed in the Security Council that something needed to be done to prevent the Serbs from ethnically cleansing Srebrenica through brute force. But in the rushed decision-making, necessitated by the town's imminent fall, the Council agreed on creating a safe area without specifying what the 'area' was and how its safety could be achieved. The resolution masked, but did not resolve, any of the fundamental differences of opinion regarding the establishment of safe areas.

For some members of the Security Council, in particular Venezuela, Pakistan and Morocco, Resolution 819 was a first step towards a wider safe-area policy, something for which they had been arguing since the Mock–Sommaruga proposal of the previous autumn. Ultimately, these countries wanted the proposal to lead to UN military intervention on the side of the Bosnian Muslims. But a majority of the Council disagreed with their ambitions.

The member states whose troops were most likely to have to implement the Council's decision, such as Britain, France and Spain, remained nervous. These countries were not prepared to be pushed into a war with the Serbs by countries that were not contributing troops to UNPROFOR. They made sure that Srebrenica was turned into a 'safe area', as opposed to a 'safe haven', the latter being what was created for the Kurds in Iraq. The difference under international law was that safe havens need not depend on consent of the warring parties and could be enforced, while safe areas were based on consent.

Still, Resolution 819 created high expectations. Many, both in Bosnia and elsewhere, believed that the United Nations from now on would protect Srebrenica against the Serbs. In reality, the resolution carefully avoided creating new military obligations for UNPROFOR either to establish or even to protect the safe area. The Council firmly placed the onus on the Serbs and the Muslims to make Srebrenica safe. UNPROFOR's role would simply be to 'monitor' the humanitarian situation.

As for the response to the resolution by UNPROFOR itself, confusion reigned. Generals Wahlgren and Morillon had great difficulty interpreting the resolution and working out a practical application. The two generals arranged to meet at Sarajevo airport with General Halilović and General Mladić at noon local time, six hours after the resolution was passed. Wahlgren and Morillon wanted to discuss a ceasefire as a first step. Mladić arrived half an hour late in a boisterous mood. His army was on the verge of completing the conquest of the enclave. He believed that he had come to accept the surrender of the town. His arrogant posturing greatly angered Morillon, who expected to negotiate but was not in a position to do so without Mladić's cooperation. Morillon's frustration was heightened because of his sense of personal commitment to Srebrenica and its people. At one point, surprising even his own side, he threatened to make a public declaration calling on Karadžić to relieve Mladić of his command.

Halilović, on the contrary, remained calm and did not respond to Mladić's provocations. He had just received a secret report from Naser Orić in Srebrenica:

> The situation was more favourable on the front lines. Some ammunition that I sent reached them and they said they would be able to hold the lines for a couple of days more. It encouraged me . . .[3]

Halilović staunchly refused to agree to surrender the enclave to the Serbs. He would only go so far as conceding that the Muslim forces in Srebrenica would 'submit' their arms to UNPROFOR.

At 02.00 on 18 April, after fourteen hours of negotiations, Mladić and Halilović reached agreement. A ceasefire would begin at 05.00 and there would be a freezing of 'all combat actions on the achieved lines of confrontation'. Canadian peacekeepers would be allowed to enter the enclave six hours later to oversee the disarming of the Muslims and facilitate the ceasefire. The Muslims had to hand in their weapons within seventy-two hours of the arrival of the Canadians in the enclave. An estimated 500 seriously wounded and sick would be allowed to leave the enclave by helicopter.

Jeremy Brade, an adviser to Owen and Thorvald Stoltenberg (who had replaced Cyrus Vance in the peacemakers' team), pointed out to Lord Owen that, fortunately, Mladić's demand that Muslim soldiers surrender to the Serbs had been kept out of the agreement. But Brade feared that 'the correct treatment of Muslim men' by the Serbs would remain a major problem. He also foresaw difficulties with the proper definition of the area for demilitarization, the completion of demilitarization within seventy-two hours, the exchange of Muslim and Serb prisoners, and the maintenance of the 'safe area' by limited UN troops. Indeed, all of these issues were to bedevil the Srebrenica enclave until the Serbs implemented their 'final solution' of July 1995.

A working group, chaired by Brigadier Vere Hayes, Morillon's British chief of staff, was instituted to flesh out the details of the agreement and deal with its implementation. Hayes faced two immediate problems. Which area was to be demilitarized and could demilitarization be achieved within seventy-two hours? Both issues were cleverly addressed in a single solution. By keeping the area of demilitarization limited to the town of Srebrenica itself, Muslim forces could move to areas under their control outside the town and avoid being disarmed. Thereby, UNPROFOR and the Canadians were absolved from a difficult task, at least for the moment. This also meant that demilitarization could be achieved quickly. In Zagreb on 21 April, just before the deadline ran out, General Wahlgren announced that demilitarization had been completed: 'From reports I have received from my officers in Srebrenica I can confirm that from noon today the town has been demilitarized.' The Serbs continued to dispute this claim while the Muslims insisted they had complied with the UN's demand.

In fact, the UN never tried systematically to disarm the Muslims in Srebrenica. On 23 April, Kofi Annan, the UN's Under-Secretary-General for Peacekeeping Operations, sent a confidential message to General Wahlgren to prepare him for a visit by a Security Council delegation, headed by the Venezuelan ambassador, Diego Arria. Annan indicated that the demilitarization of Srebrenica need not be pursued too actively:

> Given your public statements that Srebrenica is fully demilitarized, we see no need for UNPROFOR to participate in house-to-house searches for weapons. You will undoubtedly be made aware by the visiting Security Council delegation of the strong feeling amongst several Member States that UNPROFOR should not participate too actively in 'disarming the victims'.

In Srebrenica itself, a silent crowd had witnessed the entry of the Canadians into their town on 17 April. Although the shelling had stopped and they felt a little safer, their feeling of isolation did not subside. They were hungry and tired and had no water. More than 90 per cent of the children had scabies. Besides, the size and equipment of the Canadian unit was not impressive. The Canadians only numbered 143 men. Their heaviest weapons were .50-calibre machine guns. Nor did they look very confident themselves. Was this small group of lightly armed soldiers going to protect the people of Srebrenica against Mladić? The local authorities had at first been relieved by the announcement that Srebrenica had been turned into a safe area, but now they were no longer so sure. They were worried about the demilitarization negotiations. While they were asked to hand in their weapons and allow people to be evacuated, the Serbs held all the military cards.

Across the Atlantic, meanwhile, the Canadian government had begun to wonder what it had let itself and its troops in for. When Canada had been asked to offer troops to help stabilize the situation around Srebrenica, the Canadian government had agreed. It was under the impression that, as Resolution 819 seemed to imply, the task of the Canadians would be strictly humanitarian in nature. But within two days of the arrival of the Canadian troops in Srebrenica, their government smelt a rat and began to express deep misgivings about the nature of their mission. Canadian Foreign Minister Barbara McDougal telephoned her British colleague Douglas Hurd and warned him that the Canadians did not have the resources to deal with demilitarization and would be unable to prevent a breakdown of the ceasefire. In New York, Canadian officials pointed out that the situation of their troops was precarious. If demilitarization failed, the Serbs might resume attacking Srebrenica, or Muslim forces might fire on UN forces, hoping that the Serbs would be held responsible. On the other hand, if the demilitarization did take place, it would be very embarrassing if the Canadians were forced to withdraw at some point in the future, leaving disarmed Muslims to face the Serbs.

The Canadian government concluded that the UN presence in Srebrenica had to be internationalized and asked for British and French reinforcements. Neither country was keen. But, in an attempt to assuage Canadian concerns, the British government unilaterally promised to give air support to the Canadians in Srebrenica if they were to come under attack from the Serbs.

On 8 May 1993, Mladić and Halilović signed an agreement extending the demilitarized area around Srebrenica to 'within the current lines of conflict'. The Serbs agreed to withdraw their infantry 1·5 kilometres from the confrontation line and to keep their tanks and artillery 'in limited areas' that would be monitored by UNPRO-FOR, after the Muslims had handed in their weapons. However, although the town of Srebrenica had ostensibly been demilitarized, the Muslims kept most of their weapons. The Serbs refused to withdraw. An uneasy stalemate ensued.

The Muslims 'submitted' two tanks, an armoured personnel carrier, twenty-three artillery pieces and mortars, as well as some 260 small arms to the Canadians. The tanks and artillery had fired their last shells during the battle for Srebrenica. Without ammunition these weapons were useless. The tanks, moreover, no longer had any fuel. During the last two days of the battle for Srebrenica one of them had been used: its engine had been run on a mixture of thinner and transformer oil.

While the situation in Srebrenica remained tense, this was not obvious from a distance. As soon as the Serb conquest of the enclave had stopped, the media and the politicians had focused their attention on the Muslim–Croat war that flared up in central Bosnia. But the safety of the enclave was by no means assured. Declaring Srebrenica a safe area was a stop-gap measure which only succeeded in thwarting the Serbs for the interim.

Despite the fact that the success of the Srebrenica safe-area format was still an open question, the Bosnian government soon asked the UN to turn other towns in Bosnia into safe areas. Bosnia's supporters in the European Community and the Security Council took up the request and began to call for an expansion of the concept. At a meeting of the EC foreign ministers in Copenhagen on 24 April, the Netherlands argued that the Security Council should pass a resolution creating additional safe 'havens'. The new French government, led by Prime Minister Edouard Balladur, was also interested in safe areas and told its European partners that in Paris a wider safe-area policy was under serious review. With France beginning to alter its position on safe areas, the international support for the safe-area concept became considerably stronger than it had been in November 1992. In the beginning of May, after returning from their visit to UNPROFOR, the Venezuelan and Pakistani ambassadors to the UN prepared a new resolution to create additional safe areas.

The response to the resolution being prepared by Venezuela and

Pakistan had much to do with the attitude to the Vance–Owen Peace Plan. The new Clinton administration did not like the Vance–Owen plan. The US ambassador to the UN, Madeleine Albright, stated in a press conference on 24 February 1993 that the plan amounted to 'rewarding aggression and punishing the victims'. Albright reflected a strongly moralistic strand in the American debate on Bosnia. Its adherents, logically, advocated a tough, interventionist policy. But they found themselves opposed by another group in the Clinton administration who regarded Bosnia as an intractable Vietnam-like quagmire. One member of this second group, General Colin Powell, conveyed the tension of this clash in his account of a policy-making meeting:

> The debate exploded at one session when Madeleine Albright ... asked me in frustration, 'What's the point of having this superb military that you're always talking about if we can't use it?' I thought I would have an aneurysm. American GIs were not toy soldiers to be moved around on some sort of global game board.[4]

Largely as a result of these deep divisions, the Clinton administration was unable to develop a coherent policy for dealing with Bosnia.

When the resolution prepared by Venezuela and Pakistan, which extended the safe-area concept to Sarajevo, Žepa, Tuzla, Goražde and Bihać, came before the Security Council as Resolution 824, Albright voted in favour. That same day, she also conspicuously refused to support a French draft resolution endorsing the Vance–Owen plan, because, she said, the US had 'other measures' in mind.

In fact it was not so much that the US had other measures in mind but that it simply wanted to get rid of the Vance–Owen plan. Whereas Albright believed the Vance–Owen plan was immoral, many members of the CIA and the State Department, including Albright's boss, Secretary of State Warren Christopher, believed that the plan was unimplementable. Particularly in regard to eastern Bosnia, where Srebrenica lay, Christopher did not think that there was much chance of the Bosnian government ever regaining control over this territory. By mid-May, he had decided that a new peace process was needed that took into account 'the reality on the ground'. Only then could an eventual peace settlement be implemented.

Christopher began talking about 'the failed VOPP scenario' on a visit to Europe on 6 May 1993 – four days after his old boss Cyrus Vance had retired from the peacemakers' team and was replaced by the Norwegian Thorvald Stoltenberg. What Christopher wanted was to simplify the map. The Vance–Owen plan was too complicated. It did not split Bosnia into three territorially contiguous parts. On the other hand, Christopher opposed safe areas as an unworkable idea and told the Europeans as much on the very day that Albright voted for the resolution creating new safe areas. Christopher insisted that 'air power would not protect the safe areas, for which very large ground forces were needed', adding that 'there could be no question of putting US troops at risk or of needing to be rescued from the Serbs, as was happening to the Canadians in Srebrenica.'[5]

An implementation of the Vance–Owen plan required close Euro-American cooperation. Implementation implied a willingness to impose the plan on one or more of the warring parties. For that, a substantial American troop contribution was needed. But the Americans had consistently ruled that out. Serious transatlantic tensions had resulted. These tensions were of particular concern to the British, who valued their 'special relationship' with the United States. Now that the Americans had withdrawn their support for the Vance–Owen plan altogether, the British felt they had no choice but to abandon it as well. They did not want to impose it together with only the French. Just before Christopher arrived in Europe, British Foreign Secretary Douglas Hurd began to backpedal. Ironically, it was at this time in early May 1993, after months of stalling, that the Bosnian Serb leader, Radovan Karadžić, finally signed the peace deal. Needing an escape route, the British government maintained that implementation of the agreement would not start 'until the character of the peace was clearer'.[6] With both American and British support for the Vance–Owen plan withdrawn, the plan was effectively dead. Like the Americans, the British now needed an alternative strategy to promote.

In point of fact, relations between Britain and the US had become strained. The British were fed up with US pressure for them to be tougher with the Serbs, given that US ground troops remained safely at home. The proposals that the US *was* prepared to back with their own military force the British found irresponsible and dangerous. They would escalate the war without bringing any nearer the prospect of a settlement. The advocacy by the Clinton administration of a 'lift and strike' strategy – lifting the arms embargo for the Bosnian Muslims and striking the Serbs from the air with US air power – would mean putting British and other UN troops on the ground at great risk. The British also believed that there was little chance of success. The Serbs might well refuse to back down and just dig in more firmly. The Clinton administration was forced to admit privately that it had no guarantee against this contingency, and the President eventually abandoned the idea. But the acrimony over 'lift and strike' had significantly contributed to the souring of Anglo-American relations. Both sides realized they needed a strategy they could promote in concert. Neither Bosnia, nor the Vance–Owen Peace Plan, was worth a transatlantic crisis.

Yet, following the abandonment of 'lift and strike', the Vance–Owen plan, as Owen himself had said earlier, was 'the only act in town'. A new comprehensive plan could not be devised overnight. In need of a quick solution, Britain and the US turned, in an instance of willy-nilly diplomacy, towards the safe-area concept.

In fact it was the new *French* government, itself anxious to be seen to be 'doing something', which was the first of the permanent Security Council countries to promote safe areas. On 10 May 1993, France had presented the US, the UK and Russia with a draft paper on the subject. The paper was meant to serve as the basis for a new Security Council resolution on how to implement the wider safe-area policy of Resolution 824. The French paper, when it appeared in its final form on 19 May, distinguished a 'light option' and a 'heavy option'.[7] In the light option, based on the Srebrenica model, some 9,600 troops would be based in the six enclaves 'to deter aggression' through their presence. In the heavy option, 35,000 to 40,000 troops would 'oppose any aggression'.

On 13 May, the French Foreign Minister, Alain Juppé, informed journalists of the safe-areas paper. He only spoke vaguely about 'sanctuarizing' the safe areas with 10,000 to 12,000 troops. He said that these forces could not be French or British, but ought to be Russian and American. He emphasized that there was 'no question of reconquering territory occupied by the Serbs, nor of providing complete armed protection around the designated safe areas'.[8] One could detect in these statements the same uneasiness which had led Christopher and, subsequently, Hurd to abandon the Vance–Owen plan. Like his US and British colleagues, Juppé was looking for a less dangerous alternative – a stop-gap.

From this point on, the pieces came together with amazing speed. On 17 May, Warren Christopher and his press-relations adviser drafted a list of points over dinner in a Washington restaurant. It soon became known as the 'Joint Action Programme' – in which safe areas figured prominently. Basically the programme restated the policies that were already being implemented. The only shift was that the US now proposed the establishment of safe areas and of a War Crimes Tribunal. The programme was quickly backed by both the French and the British.

At the last minute, the Russian Foreign Minister, Andrei Kozyrev, threatened to complicate matters. Kozyrev had been stirred into action by the French paper on the safe areas. He wanted to call an extraordinary Security Council meeting of the four foreign ministers in New York to discuss the idea further. Kozyrev's enthusiasm for the French safe-area initiative worried Christopher. The Secretary of State did not want to concede the initiative to the Russians and be drawn into a commitment to a 'heavier' safe-area policy. Instead of going to meet Kozyrev in New York, Christopher asked him to come to Washington.

Kozyrev went to Washington on 20 May. He saw the establishment of safe areas as the start of a phased implementation of the Vance–Owen plan. During a long meeting with Christopher, Kozyrev realized that this was not at all what the Americans had in mind. He was finally persuaded to accept the American draft text by the promise that the Bosnian Serbs would be allowed a large territorially contiguous part of eastern Bosnia and a northern corridor that would allow them to connect Serbia proper to Serb-held territory in Croatia and western Bosnia. This was something the Russians had long argued should happen. News of the Russians' agreement was then immediately leaked to *The New York Times*, making it impossible for Kozyrev to distance himself from the accord.

Douglas Hurd and Alain Juppé arrived in New York on 21 May. The Spanish Foreign Minister, Javier Solana, was also invited.[9] The five ministers formally signed the 'Joint Action Programme' the next day. Subsequently, the programme was presented to the UN Security Council as a common position of the five member states. But, though the US, Russia, Britain, France and Spain agreed to create safe areas, the terms of the programme made it clear they did not intend to give the areas any 'teeth'. This became even clearer in the ensuing debate over the upcoming Security Council resolution that would address the question of how to implement the wider safe-area policy of Resolution 824 of 6 May.

Despite the efforts of the 'non-aligned' countries within the Security Council, who had been working since the publication of the French paper to secure the strongest possible support for the Bosnian Muslims, it soon became clear that the 'heavy' safe-area option would not be adopted.

In the Security Council, the conflict between the Joint Action Programme five and the non-aligned countries came to a head on 2 June, when Ambassador Jesus of Cape Verde read out a long statement on behalf of the non-aligned movement. Jesus declared that the non-aligned countries disagreed with the Joint Action Programme because it lacked a commitment to reverse Serbian aggression and was not linked to the Vance–Owen plan. The next day, the non-aligned group presented the Joint Action Programme signatories with a draft safe-area resolution of their own, in which all Muslim and Croat areas as designated by the Vance–Owen plan came under UN protection. This was far too bold a step for the signatories of the Joint Action Programme.

When the non-aligned group realized that the joint action signatories were never going to support their proposal, they dropped it and began to try to toughen up the resolution drafted by France, inserting language that would put an end to the UN's impartiality. Yet the joint action signatories insisted on inserting crucial phrases that sufficiently weakened the language of the resolution and exempted their ground troops from the obligation to enforce the safety of the safe areas. Finally, on 4 June, a text was more or less agreed, and it was adopted as Resolution 836.

Like Resolution 819, Resolution 836 was inherently contradictory and open to a variety of interpretations. This was the first resolution on Bosnia that referred to Chapter VII of the UN Charter without any qualification, which meant that, in the implementation of the safe-area policy, UNPROFOR was no longer acting under a peacekeeping mandate but under a peace-enforcing mandate. Much of the remainder of the text sounded equally tough. Closer scrutiny revealed, however, that all was not quite as it seemed. The two most important paragraphs were 5 and 9. In paragraph 5 the Security Council 'extended' the mandate of UNPROFOR to enable it

> to deter attacks against the safe areas, to monitor the ceasefire [and] to promote the withdrawal of military or paramilitary units other than those of the Government of the Republic of Bosnia and Herzegovina . . .

The non-aligned countries had wanted UNPROFOR to 'defend' the safe areas, but the Joint Action Programme five had stuck to the term 'deter'. As a consolation, the non-aligned had been allowed to insert language allowing the Bosnian government's troops to stay inside the safe areas. By allowing the Bosnian forces to remain, the UN Security Council was symbolically siding with the Bosnian government. Yet paragraph 9 complicated this:

> [The Security Council] authorizes UNPROFOR . . . in carrying out the mandate defined in paragraph 5 above, acting in self-defence, to take the necessary measures, including the use of force, in reply to bombardments against the safe areas by any of the parties or to armed incursion into them or in the event of any deliberate obstruction in or around those areas to the freedom of movement of UNPROFOR or of protected humanitarian convoys.

A first reading of the paragraph made it seem that UN troops deployed inside safe areas would have to use force in reply to Serb attacks. However, at the insistence of the British, French and Spanish, the qualification 'acting in self-defence' had been inserted into the text. These words, in combination with the fact that UNPROFOR's main task was limited to 'deterrence', instead of 'defence', ensured that there was no obligation for the UN troops involved in implementing the safe-area policy to use force against the Serbs unless and until UNPROFOR itself was under direct threat.

Shashi Tharoor, Special Assistant to the UN Under-Secretary-General for Peacekeeping Operations, commented dryly on the safe-area resolutions in an article he later wrote:

The Security Council resolutions on the safe areas required the parties to treat them as 'safe', imposed no obligations on their inhabitants and defenders, deployed United Nations troops in them but expected their mere presence to 'deter attacks', carefully avoided asking the peacekeepers to 'defend' or 'protect' these areas, but authorized them to call in air power 'in self-defence' – a masterpiece of diplomatic drafting, but largely unimplementable as an operational directive.[10]

As for what lessons might be learned in June 1993 from the already existing safe area, Srebrenica, a confidential UNHCR report painfully exposed the gap between the reality in Srebrenica and the safe-area concept under discussion in New York:

> Once the focus shifts from the establishment of the safe areas and the basic rehabilitation of the people trapped in these areas it will become – as is already the case in Srebrenica – evident to the population that there is no plan for their future and that they face a life of enforced idleness in a refugee camp. Frustration and aggressivity will rise, possibly jeopardizing the demilitarization process . . .
>
> Although safer from shelling than it has been in over a year, the social situation [in Srebrenica] is worsening daily as basic survival needs are not met. Violence, black-market activities, prostitution, theft are becoming the only activities of the population. Tensions are mounting between the majority refugee population and minority local population. As always the women, children and elderly are most at risk. The enclave must now be recognized for what it is, namely a closed refugee camp of 50,000 persons without adequate facilities for more than about 15,000.

Warnings like these fell on deaf ears. Safe areas had begun to serve a 'greater' political interest than the actual needs of the beleaguered people of Srebrenica and the other five Bosnian towns.

Now that the Security Council had decided to create additional safe areas, one final issue remained outstanding: finding the troops. In preparation for an official report from the Secretary-General, General Wahlgren was asked to assess the number of troops needed to implement Resolution 836. Wahlgren was very unhappy about the resolution. The day before it passed the Council, he had sent a warning to New York. The clause in the resolution which allowed the Bosnian Army to stay in the safe areas worried him particularly:

> If one allowed no controls of the military or paramilitary units of the Bosnian government, one would create a scenario which would encourage the use of safe areas as havens where forces could refit, rearm, train and prepare for further military operations. The history of the Vietnam conflict immediately comes to mind.

Wahlgren feared that the safe areas would intensify the war. Moreover, they would be likely to invite attacks from the Serbs, whom it would be hard to convince they were still being treated 'impartially' by the UN. To deter them would clearly require massive numbers of UN troops.

To 'effectively deter' attacks against the safe areas, Wahlgren argued that 34,000 troops were necessary. The forces already in Bosnia were stretched to the limit, so this number was in addition to existing strength.

But the Joint Action Programme five would have none of it. Wahlgren's request for 34,000 was 'excessive'. The Secretariat of the UN was told to focus instead on a 'light' option, as proposed in the French paper of May, which required fewer than 10,000 soldiers.

On 14 June, the Secretary-General's report on how to implement Resolution 836 was ready. It stated that, although 34,000 extra troops were needed if UNPROFOR was to effectively deter attacks against the safe areas, a 'basic level of deterrence' could be provided with a reinforcement of 7,600 troops. Four days later, the Council adopted Resolution 844, authorizing a reinforcement of UNPROFOR with the lower number.

Yet by the time Resolution 844 was adopted it had already become painfully clear that assembling even 7,600 troops was not going to be possible. A long line of nations refused to contribute any forces at all, beginning with the Spanish. The French made it clear that they wanted to concentrate their troops in Bihać and Sarajevo 'for their own security' and that they would not take on a third safe area. (Later the French withdrew from Bihać altogether.) The Americans stuck to the position they had already staked out in May, when President Clinton indicated that the US would provide air support for the safe areas but ruled out sending ground troops into a 'shooting gallery'. The British government politely informed the UN Secretariat that they wanted British troops to remain within their current areas of operation in central Bosnia. Russia, noting the lack of enthusiasm among its joint action partners, also refused to take part. Subsequently the Scandinavians, who had initially been positive, also decided not to contribute troops. The UN Secretariat was in danger of exhausting its list. Though the Canadians were still in Srebrenica, the French were in Bihać and Sarajevo and some British troops were in Tuzla, no country seemed willing to replace the Canadians or take on either of the two remaining eastern enclaves. Except for the Netherlands.

NOTES

1. Voorhoeve also advocated these ideas internationally: see *International Herald Tribune*, 11 August 1992.

2. Anet Bleich, 'Safe havens in Bosnië: een zinnig voorstel' ('Safe havens in Bosnia: a sensible proposal'), *De Volkskrant*, 24 November 1992.

3. Interview with Sefer Halilović, carried out for the television series *The Death of Yugoslavia*, produced by Angus Macqueen, Paul Mitchell and Norma Percy for Brian Lapping Associates, 1995, Liddell Hart Centre for Military Archives, King's College, London.

4. Colin Powell, *My American Journey* (New York: Ballantine Books, 1996), p. 561.

5. Owen, *Balkan Odyssey*, p. 160.

6. Owen, *Balkan Odyssey*, p. 152.

7. The light option also contained a light-light option, whereby UNPROFOR would only deploy monitors in the safe areas.

8. Owen, *Balkan Odyssey*, p. 165.

9. Britain and France, aware they were breaking ground-rules of EC diplomacy, decided to bring in Spain. Spain was on the Security Council and had shown itself to be a reliable partner over Bosnia, opposing safe areas during the debate in 1992 and ruling out a military intervention with ground forces.

10. Shashi Tharoor, 'Should UN peacekeeping go "back to basics"?' *Survival*, Vol. 37, No. 4 (Winter 1995–6), p. 60.

CHAPTER SIX

'A Principled Course':
The Dutch and Srebrenica

On 2 November 1993, a letter arrived at the Dutch Ministry of Defence in The Hague from the UN Secretary-General Boutros-Ghali. He wrote that he now wanted to take up the offer made by the Dutch government a few months earlier, when the UN had requested combat troops for the protection of the safe areas. The letter caused great consternation at the ministry. No one could remember the Netherlands having made such a commitment. On searching through records, however, civil servants soon discovered that indeed they had. It was Defence Minister Relus ter Beek who, while visiting New York on 7 September, had offered Boutros-Ghali a battalion of the new airmobile brigade and had not excluded safe areas as its possible area of deployment.[1] And now, despite serious reservations among the military, the ministry could not renege on its promise. The Netherlands was thus the only Western UN member state to respond positively to the Secretariat's June 1993 request for troops to implement the Security Council safe-area resolutions. The Dutch were moving inexorably towards Srebrenica.

'Peacekeeping' was extremely popular in the Netherlands. Government, parliament and people alike strongly supported the concept. Ministers always found a receptive audience when they spoke of 'the gross injustice' being committed in the former Yugoslavia and the moral obligation of the Netherlands to help end the conflict. At its high point, in early 1994, around 3,100 Dutch troops were deployed in and around the former Yugoslavia – in relative terms by far the largest contribution among NATO countries and, in absolute terms, the third largest (after France and the United Kingdom). All of these deployments – including to Srebrenica – were approved by unanimous votes in parliament.

As for the brief of these troops, the government had erred on the side of caution. Their primary role was to provide humanitarian relief. Also, it was believed that their presence, along with the other UN troops, had 'a certain dampening effect' on the extent or severity of human-rights violations. Finally, the troops might 'contribute to the creation of the necessary preconditions' for a durable peace. The success of at least the humanitarian effort, the government claimed, was proved by the fact that civilian casualties had dropped from 130,000 in 1992 to 13,000 in 1994.

In fact, the popular view of the conflict supported much more robust intervention. The consensus opinion was that the Serbs and Serbian aggression were the guilty party. A majority of Dutch believed that this guilty party should not just be contained but punished, and polls consistently indicated that the Dutch people favoured peace-*enforcement* in Bosnia. At the end of 1992, 66 per cent supported Dutch participation in a military intervention and accepted that it would involve Dutch casualties.[2] An endless stream of op-eds in the major newspapers reinforced this view.

Prominent figures in calling for military intervention were the former supporters of the massive anti-nuclear protest movement of the early 1980s. Their strong moral commitment to nuclear disarmament now transferred itself to combating injustice and human-rights abuses in the former Yugoslavia. At the end of 1992, Mient-Jan Faber, a former leader of the anti-nuclear campaign, helped organize 'contemplation meetings' in churches around the country where he 'confessed his own guilt'. At these meetings, he argued that by not offering protection to cities such as Sarajevo and Srebrenica, where tens of thousands of people were trapped and exposed to 'the terror bombardments of the Četniks, the international community was also guilty of this form of genocide'.

Faber strongly supported the safe-haven concept. In early 1993, mimicking a highly successful form of protest from the heady days of his crusade against nuclear missiles, he helped organize a national 'postcard action'. Faber presented negotiators Lord Owen and Cyrus Vance in Geneva with more than 157,000 postcards demanding the establishment of safe havens in Bosnia:

We visited Owen in January 1993 with people from Sarajevo

and Belgrade and Zagreb. He said that it was the silliest idea he'd ever heard ... and four months later it was adopted by the Security Council![3]

High moral calls for action were not, however, the exclusive domain of the activist left. Joris Voorhoeve, former leader of the main conservative party and, at the time, head of the international relations think-tank 'Clingendael', fundamentally agreed with Faber: 'For Evil to be victorious the only requirement is for good people to do nothing.'[4] In a flurry of op-eds, Voorhoeve called for military intervention and the establishment of safe havens.

A majority of Dutch MPs greatly sympathized with the theoretical calls for more robust action in Bosnia and pressed the government to drum up international support. However, when the parliament turned to the subject of the actual role of Dutch peacekeepers, MPs' views suddenly reflected more restraint. They expressed great concern about the well-being and security of the Dutch troops and constantly pressed ministers for more information. What was their pay like? Were their leave provisions and living conditions adequate? What would happen if soldiers ended up with disabilities? Would they be properly looked after? Above all, were the men and women safe? The government's standard answer was not to worry, the Dutch troops were running no more than 'a well-considered and acceptable risk'. The danger that this risk might grow *un*acceptable if the stakes were raised was something that was certain to give the politicians pause.

The call for more robust action ran into a practical problem as well: the Dutch had no combat troops readily available. The army was still conscript-based, and conscripts could not be sent on peacekeeping missions without their consent, and even then, as Prime Minister Ruud Lubbers once remarked, they could change their minds 'on the steps into the aircraft'. Although conscription was to be abolished by 1998, the army had not yet completed the formation of any all-volunteer combat units. The Royal Navy possessed some professional marines' units, but these were already serving with the UN in Cambodia. The first all-volunteer army unit – a battalion of the army's new crack troops, the airmobile brigade – would not be ready until November 1993. So the units that were first sent into former Yugoslavia were a signals battalion, in March 1992, and a transport battalion, in November 1992.

The issue of eventually sending army combat units did not go away, however. The Dutch foreign ministry believed it was a good idea. Such units would improve the 'visibility' of Dutch foreign policy. Foreign ministry officials were greatly frustrated by their exclusion from the international forums that sought solutions to the conflict. Since they believed that the dominant voices of these debates favoured the Serbs too heavily and as a result rewarded aggression, the Dutch foreign ministry felt a pressing need for their voice to be heard. Combat units might open the doors of international diplomacy to them.

But the Dutch Ministry of Defence was hesitant, based on the advice of its top soldiers, in particular the chief of defence staff, General Arie van der Vlis, and the Commander of Land Forces, Lieutenant-General Hans Couzy. They had three major concerns.

The first was of a bureaucratic nature. Participation in peacekeeping was not in the institutional self-interest of the army because it compromised equipment plans. The airmobile brigade was slotted to receive some sixty new combat and transport helicopters by the end of the century. 'What went through my mind,' General Van der Vlis later said, 'was the question: will this not mean the end of the airmobile brigade? Because people would perhaps start saying: "See, they can work very well with armour. We don't need those helicopters." '[5] Van der Vlis and others feared that what was to become the jewel in the Dutch army's crown would be taken away.

Second, Van der Vlis and Couzy both believed that the Dutch army was not ready yet. It needed more time to complete the transition from a conscript-based to a professional army. They believed it would take several years at least for the forces to acquire the culture and ethos of a professional military.

Third, the generals were afraid of being sucked into an unwinnable guerrilla conflict. General Couzy was exceptionally outspoken on this issue. He described the nature of the Bosnian conflict on a radio programme in January 1993:

I have seen the country, I have seen the warring parties and I know their history. If you want to force a military solution on the ground, you need a large force of 100,000 to 200,000 soldiers. This is only possible if America is prepared to participate. But the US has said already that it is unwilling. Europe does not have the capability to supply so many troops. If one decided to enter into ground combat in spite of this, it would stir up a hornet's nest. It will be necessary to commit more troops again and again, and ultimately you have to imagine a Vietnam scenario.

In fact, the prospect of becoming entangled in a second Vietnam, whether justified or not, haunted all the NATO militaries. Safe areas would bring this nightmare closer, as Van der Vlis had argued on national television, because they implied taking sides in the conflict. Notably in the United States and Britain, such fears had succeeded in convincing the national governments that intervention was not a good idea. In the Netherlands, the military failed in its effort to achieve a similar recognition by its own government and, in the end, the pressure to commit combat troops was too great for the soldiers and their minister to withstand.

During 1993, pressure in Parliament for more action increased. The Labour Party, which was part of the governing coalition, was particularly exasperated by the failure of the international community to combat what they perceived as *the* major injustice of the war: the ethnic cleansing of the Bosnian Muslims. So when the Security Council adopted Resolution 824 and declared six safe areas in Bosnia in May, the Dutch parliament immediately pressed the government to support the initiative with combat troops. On 19 May 1993, a joint Labour–Christian Democrat parliamentary motion was carried which called on the government 'to prepare the airmobile brigade for action in anticipated UN operations'.

In June 1993, when the UN began its search for 34,000 troops for the safe areas, the Dutch government did volunteer a battalion of the airmobile brigade – though not yet for deployment in the safe areas. The Ministry of Defence's opposition had managed at least to secure this stipulation.

However, when Defence Minister Ter Beek met UN Secretary-General Boutros-Ghali on 7 September 1993 and formally offered the 11th battalion of the airmobile brigade to the UN to be deployed 'in support of a peace settlement', he failed to clearly state that safe areas were excluded as an alternative destination. In fact, Defence Ministry officials were not aware that five days before Ter Beek's visit, the Dutch ambassador to the UN, Niek Biegman, had already promised troops for the safe areas. According to a 1996 Foreign Ministry letter to the Dutch parliament, Biegman had told the Under-Secretary-General for Peacekeeping Operations, Kofi Annan, on 2 September 1993 that

> the Netherlands had already in June offered to participate in a force for the 'safe areas' [with a logistics unit]. This offer had not (yet) been effectuated, because UN requirements ... did not match Dutch possibilities. The Netherlands remained prepared, however, to participate in the 'safe area' implementation and would be able in January 1994 to offer a battalion of the airmobile brigade, including a logistical component ...

These troop offers were intended by the Foreign Ministry as a 'catalyst' to inspire other countries to do their bit.

By November 1993, in the absence of a peace settlement, safe areas seemed the most likely candidate for Dutch troop deployment. As this reality dawned, opinion in the Netherlands began to waver. Support for tough action against the Serbs turned out to be not so strong after all. MPs now nervously asked for clarification on the rules of engagement and questioned whether the battalion was properly equipped.

The government was quick to play down the dangers. Foreign Minister Peter Kooijmans and Defence Minister Ter Beek wrote in a joint letter to Parliament:

> The rules of engagement for the additional Dutch blue helmets are the same as those of the other UN units in Bosnia-Herzegovina. These permit the use of force as a final resort in self-defence and if a UN unit is forcibly prevented from carrying out its tasks.

The tension in the Dutch position, which wavered between an unwillingness to run risks and the desire for tougher action, shone through in the letter. Towards the end, summarizing the policy regarding the rules of engagement, the ministers wrote, in a sentence full of qualifiers, that the airmobile battalion's operations could 'if necessary, be more robust'.

It was while General Van der Vlis was on holiday that the army top command had agreed to make the airmobile battalion available for Bosnia. What had swayed the debate was the belief of some generals that such an assignment would benefit the army's image. An extensive television and billboard advertising campaign had emphasized the exciting opportunities offered by the new, all-volunteer, red beret airmobile brigade. It would be unfortunate if the brigade, as one general put it, 'got no further than . . . a little exercise in Greece'.[6] That said, even the pro-deployment generals had not favoured the eastern enclaves.

Defence Minister Ter Beek and the Commander of Land Forces, General Couzy, travelled on a fact-finding mission to Bosnia from 9 to 11 November 1993. Ter Beek repeatedly stressed to the UN commanders that he did not want the Dutch to be sent to the safe areas, and for a while, it looked like the battalion might not end up in a safe area after all. That same month, the situation in central Bosnia had much deteriorated, and a reinforced UN presence might be needed to separate the fighting Croats and Muslims; this job might fall to the Dutch. By late November, however, it became clear this was not going to happen, and the safe areas of Srebrenica and Žepa were assigned to the Dutch unit. On a reconnaissance mission to the region, the Deputy Commander of Land Forces, Major-General Ruurd Reitsma, learned of the unit's destination from the UNPRO-FOR commander, Belgian Lieutenant-General Francis Briquemont. Reitsma was a keen proponent of image-enhancement for the unit. He reported back to The Hague that, in his opinion, this was 'an honourable, difficult, but do-able task'.

In The Hague, the army's top leadership agreed that, if it had to be the safe areas, the battalion must at least avoid getting caught up in real fighting. As Couzy later stated, the battalion's UN mission was 'not fighting [the Serbs] and not defending the population'.[7] Van der Vlis and Couzy set two demands. First, the Dutch unit was only to serve in Bosnia for a maximum period of eighteen months – although the UN was not informed of this until six months into the deployment. Second, the unit must always remain together and be equipped with such a combination of weapons that it would maximize self-protection and deter attacks on itself, but at the same time not be seen as a possible intervention force. Peacekeeping, according to General Van der Vlis, meant having 'just enough means to manage the situation'.

In the first instance, the general staff wanted to furnish the battalion with wheeled armoured vehicles. These were considered to be more typical of peacekeeping duties and less threatening. 'They did not look like tanks,' one senior officer noted. But the Dutch did not possess such vehicles. An attempt to lease them from Finland failed when that country set an unacceptable price. In the end, the army was forced to use their own tracked YPRs. The YPR was the mainstay of the armoured infantry battalions. They were normally armed with a 25mm cannon. Such a weapon, however, was deemed too heavy and too aggressive. Instead, the general staff chose to take a selection of YPRs that had a .50-calibre heavy machine gun in lieu of the cannon. Soldiers could also be trained more easily in the use of machine guns than the cannon, and the former required much less maintenance. The 120mm mortar battery of the battalion was considered too heavy as well and replaced, at a late stage, by six lighter, 81mm mortars. Six long-range TOW and eighteen medium-range Dragon anti-tank missile systems were taken to Srebrenica. But a unit of four light Bölkow helicopters was not allowed in by the Serbs.

All in all, the battalion was equipped very much like a traditional peacekeeping unit, which relied on the consent of the warring factions and which would need weapons and armour for self-protection and the defusion of local crises only. Dutch MPs worried that the armament was too light and some lobbied to have heavier weapons supplied. What most of them did not realize was that quantity and quality of armament mattered little if no supplies with which to use them reached the battalion. Indeed, logistics proved to be the Achilles' heel of the Srebrenica safe area. The more equipment the Dutch brought with them, the more supplies they needed – and thus the more they depended on the Serbs, who after all completely controlled all access to the enclave.

The fundamental flaw with the Dutch decision-making process regarding the deployment of combat units to Bosnia was that it was driven almost exclusively by moral outrage. The public, parliament and the government all wanted to do something about the war. But few considered carefully whether something that was actually *useful* could be achieved. Although once they were adopted, the safe-area resolutions found broad theoretical support internationally, all of the major allies baulked at actually providing the means for implementation of the resolutions. The Dutch government failed to read the negative signals emanating from their NATO allies. Naïvely they believed that by setting an example they would inspire others to follow. The safe-area resolutions had been taken by the Dutch at face value. Few seemed to realize that the actual motivation behind them was to paper over the abandonment of the Vance–Owen Peace Plan. Even when it became clear that no other Western countries were going to volunteer to send troops to the eastern enclaves, the Dutch government ignored the danger and made a lone commitment. This was especially unwise, because if the Dutch got into trouble – and there was a good chance they might – they would be dependent on other nations.

This dependence on other countries was exposed even before the mission of 'Dutchbat' had begun. In early December 1993, the battalion's forward reconnaissance party was refused entry into Srebrenica by the Serbs. Since the Serbs were also refusing the UN access to the airport near Tuzla and were stepping up the pressure on besieged Sarajevo, the situation became so serious that the issue was discussed in the 10–11 January meeting of the NATO heads of state and government. In the final communiqué, NATO threatened air strikes if the Dutch party continued to be blocked.

UN Secretary-General Boutros-Ghali was in The Hague on 19 January 1994, just before the Dutch were going to attempt to enter Srebrenica again, at the end of the month. Prime Minister Ruud Lubbers told the Secretary-General that he was concerned that the UN decision-making process for authorizing air support, particularly close air support, might not work. He asked whether the decision to call in close air support could be delegated to the military commanders on the ground. The Secretary-General rejected the idea, but he could not provide Lubbers with a viable alternative. If NATO wanted to take over the military role in Bosnia altogether, he would be happy to comply. Lubbers was astonished by the Secretary-General's flippancy. Boutros-Ghali then asserted that decisions regarding the use of air power lay with the Security Council. Later in the conversation, however, he said that the responsibility for authorizing the use of air power was his and that of his special representative, Yasushi Akashi. The contradiction surprised Lubbers, but he decided not to ask for clarification at this point, in case the Secretary-General committed himself to the option Lubbers did not want (Security Council control). Despite Boutros-Ghali's reassurance that requests for air support could be honoured within two hours, Lubbers came out of the meeting believing that there was little, if any, guarantee that the UN would provide air support if the Dutch in Srebrenica came under attack. What is more, if the Secretary-General was right in his first assertion – that the Security Council made the decision for air support – then the Dutch feared a possible Russian obstacle. Dutch diplomats requested urgent clarification from the UN Secretariat.

But this clarification was not forthcoming (air power was still a matter of heated debate between the US, France, Britain and Russia), and after a while the enthusiasm of the Dutch government for achieving it seemed to wane. This probably had much to do with a mortar attack, on 5 February 1994 in Sarajevo, which killed sixty-nine people. Following the attack NATO swiftly issued an ultimatum to the Bosnian Serbs ordering them to withdraw their artillery from a twenty-kilometre 'total exclusion zone' around Sarajevo within ten days or to face air attacks. By this time, advance parties of the Dutch battalion were deploying in Srebrenica. Although the Dutch government supported the NATO ultimatum, privately it began to worry about the vulnerability of its troops. One of the main national newspapers noted that the government's views on air power suddenly had become more 'cautious'. Foreign Minister Kooijmans now strongly advocated the involvement of the UN in decisions on the use of air power.[8] Amazingly, the Dutch preoccupation with air power seemed to have shifted from ensuring its quick deployment to preventing it from happening in too much haste.

Meanwhile, in Srebrenica Dutchbat had begun to experience the difficulties of peacekeeping in an isolated enclave. In late January 1994, the first elements of the 1,170-strong airmobile battalion arrived in Bosnia. On 3 March, some 570 Dutch troops officially relieved the 140-odd Canadian soldiers who had been in Srebrenica since April 1993. A support command, with another 350 men, was set up in Lukavac in central Bosnia. The company destined for Žepa, however, had a lucky 'escape'. It was reassigned to Simin Han in the so-called 'Sapna Thumb' in June.

From the start, the Srebrenica battalion failed to get all of their supplies into the enclave. It was particularly unlucky with ammunition. A ship carrying most of the Dutch ammunition stocks had broken down in the Gulf of Biscay. By the time it docked in Croatia, the Serbs had declared that the 250-odd container loads the Dutch had already transported into Srebrenica were more than sufficient, and they forbade any more to go through. Nine months later, some 120 containers – among them the bulk of the ammunition – were still languishing in the depot at Lukavac. By July 1995, Dutchbat only possessed 16 per cent of its operational ammunition requirement. Much of what they did have had become unreliable after eighteen months and needed replacement.

Subsequent supply convoys to Srebrenica were often delayed by the Serbs and subjected to interminable checks. Sometimes convoys were turned back. Fuel was a particularly difficult item. The Serbs took great care to keep supplies to a minimum because they knew that no modern army could properly function without them. It meant that the Dutch could not patrol the enclave in their armoured vehicles and had to go on foot instead. Other fundamental amenities also broke down. Power generators had to be switched off frequently and so there was little electricity. The conveniences of life in an affluent society – light, hot water, television and fresh food (which could not be stored without electricity to run the fridges) – conveniences which many of the Dutch soldiers assumed to be an inalienable part of their life, even if they were soldiers, were no longer a given.

Going on leave was problematic as well. The Serbs regularly refused clearance for convoys to exit the enclave, or at least held them up. In November 1994, NATO aircraft attacked a Serb airbase in Udbina and, a few days later, a number of Serb anti-aircraft missile batteries. In retaliation, seventy Dutch soldiers who were on their way home were taken hostage by the Serbs. Forbidden to use their radio communications, the outside world lost all contact with them. On the fourth day of their forced stopover, they were visited by General Mladić, who arrived in a resprayed Mercedes jeep that the Serbs had confiscated from one of the previous Dutch convoys. Dutch private Nijhuis later told an *NRC/Handelsblad* correspondent:

> He was with us for five minutes. He said to one of the chaps 'NATO' and then ran his fingers across his throat. And this

chap kept responding 'Dobro, dobro.' He did not realize that meant 'good'.[9]

After more than six days, and interventions on the highest diplomatic level, the seventy Dutch soldiers were released.

Such incidents were clearly designed to intimidate the Dutch soldiers and emphasize time and again how dependent they were on the Serbs for their well-being. None the less, the six-month tours of Dutchbat I and II in 1994 went reasonably well. Usually, the Serbs would allow supply convoys through before the situation had become too desperate.

In one of those all-too-frequent Bosnian paradoxes, the Dutch drew their beer and soft drink supplies, and occasionally pastries, from the Serbs. Once or twice a week, a small van would leave the compound in Potočari for Hotel Fontana in Bratunac. On the border of the enclave, they would pass checkpoint 'Yellow Bridge'. Warrant Officer Piet Hein Both described the scene in one of his letters to his wife:

> [At checkpoint Yellow Bridge] sits a quiet, older man. A teacher type. We have built up a very cosy relationship with him. It all revolves around this one man. An amiable person. His name is Jovo. He controls the whole lot. We supply him with electricity supplies and other things. There you are drinking rum in one of those bare containers. It is a bit like one of those films about South American gangs and I am part of it.[10]

After a drink or, if they were lucky, just coffee, the van (even in times of fuel shortages they would drive), continued to Hotel Fontana. There, after a bit of bargaining over a copious lunch, the beverages would be bought, usually some 20,000 DM worth. Occasionally, the Serbs were unable to supply the goods – which could not have surprised the Dutch excessively. After all, Serbia was subject to international sanctions. Finally, whether successful or not, the party would return 'drunk in the line of duty' past Jovo, to Potočari.

In February 1995, the Serbs proposed to expand the trade. They asked Both to mediate in the sale of goods to the Muslims. 'We can supply everything, except ammunition and weapons,' he was told. 'The same sort of business already exists in Goražde.'[11] The surprised warrant officer later found out from UNHCR that such a trade did indeed exist in the other safe area. The Srebrenica Muslims showed interest in striking a deal and sent a delegation from the war council and also the director of the soup kitchen. But the meeting fell through. After a nervous wait near Yellow Bridge, the Serb negotiators failed to turn up. On the way from Pale, so the message went, they had met with a car accident. In the middle of May, a meeting did success-fully occur. The Muslims requested information about goods and prices and agreed to meet again to place orders. But by that time, tensions around the enclave had increased to such a level that the matter was not pursued.

A large number of Muslim soldiers were encamped in the enclave. The official Bosnian Army unit was the 28th Division, which consisted of three or four brigades with a total of perhaps 1,500 active soldiers. They were armed with an odd assortment of light weapons, some machine guns, anti-tank weapons and light mortars. In times of emer-gency, in line with traditional Yugoslav military principles, more local militia could be called up for territorial defence. The total number of soldiers, UN sources estimated, was 3,000 to 4,000 men.

According to Sector North East instruction OPO 5/94, Dutchbat was 'to take all measures to maintain [the] Srebrenica ceasefire agree-ment and achieve full demilitarization of the enclave'. But despite their mandate, the Dutch made little headway in disarming the Muslims. Usually, armed Bosnians took care to disappear as soon as they noticed a Dutch patrol. The few attempts to disarm them and investigate incidents led to tense stand-offs. In January 1995, almost 100 men of Dutchbat III were taken hostage by the Bosnian Army when they investigated the fighting that had broken out in the south-western part of the enclave, in the so-called Bandera triangle. They were released after a few days, but the Dutch subsequently marked the area on their maps as suffering from 'severe restrictions of move-ment' and avoided it.

At the end of 1994, Dutchbat soldiers on patrol noted a lot of trench-digging by Muslims. The question was raised: did the trenches violate the demilitarization of the enclave? The battalion commander asked for clarification from Sector North East in Tuzla. A confidential report came back. It epitomized the nature of the mandate in general. A straightforward question did not have a straightforward answer. The demilitarization agreement of 8 May 1993 between Generals Halilović and Mladić stated that 'any military operation is strictly forbidden'. This was interpreted by the Swedish staff officer assigned to research the issue to mean that purely defensive positions were all right provided they were not 'provocative', that is, not dug within the 'security corridor', the 1·5 kilometres along the confrontation line. Yet since the confrontation line had never been reliably established (and, in practice, had moved on more than one occasion), resolution of the issue was left to the battalion commander's own judgement. By the summer of 1995, the enclave was ringed by trenches.

Though they patrolled the enclave and built more and more observation posts, the Dutch had little idea of what was going on around them. They noted frequent fighting. Complaints from the Serbs appeared to confirm that the Muslims regularly mounted raids into Serb territory to terrorize the local Serb population and acquire booty. Dutch soldiers often ran into people leaving the enclave, particularly in the direction of Žepa, fifteen kilometres to the south. They would return laden with goods, including weapons. The Dutch strongly suspected that there was a brisk trade going on between the Srebrenica Muslims and the outside world, partly in connivance with the Serbs. The enclave was certainly not hermetically sealed. UN estimates suggested that the safe area was surrounded by some three to four battalions of the Bosnian Serb Drina Corps, each consisting of some 250 locally recruited, often middle-aged men. They maintained a loose siege through artillery, roadblocks and minefields.

Dutch contact with the Bosnian Muslim population remained limited. To many of the Dutch soldiers' eyes the refugees did not offer an edifying spectacle. The enclave was overpopulated. People were underfed and badly clothed. Hygiene was a problem. Skin diseases and other illnesses were rampant. Most people had little to do. In Srebrenica and Potočari, Dutch soldiers reported being struck by the massive numbers of Muslims who 'wandered around aimlessly'. Some Dutch were shocked by the eagerness with which Muslims would await the dumping of rubbish on the tip outside the compound in order to scan it for usable items or food. Burglary in the compounds and OPs was a constant menace. Many soldiers spoke in disparaging terms of the Muslims.

On their patrols and in their observation posts, soldiers were almost always surrounded by children. In OP Golf, soldiers were woken each morning with cries of 'Hey, mister, bon bon.'[12] Some ten to fifteen children hovered around the OP during the day. This became OP Golf's only contact with the local population. In other OPs there was some barter trade with locals, but nowhere were there extensive contacts, other than with the children. Soldiers would regularly get worked up about their presence and try to chase them away.

The Dutch group that had the closest contacts with the locals was the battalion's medical unit. It supported the efforts of local doctors and the main humanitarian organization in the enclave, Médécins sans Frontières, by performing operations and holding surgeries. Some other soldiers tried to contribute something as well. Dutch explosives experts taught 'mine awareness classes' in the local schools. In one notable initiative, Dutchbat soldiers tried to rebuild the eight schools in the enclave and, via family and other contacts in the Netherlands, collected teaching materials. To maintain the impartiality of the UN, a Serb school in Bratunac was also included in the project.

In addition to patrolling, the battalion's other main task was to assist in protecting UNHCR convoys with humanitarian aid for the civilian population. These convoys came through with relative regularity. During 1994, a total of 5,858 tons were delivered by 122 convoys. This was less than the 8,916 tons of the year before, and by the end of 1994 there were increasing shortages, which led to growing tensions not only with the Muslims but also with the Serbs, because the knock-on effect was that Muslims began to mount more raids. During 1995, the aid situation improved somewhat, when, on a monthly basis, the amount of aid more than doubled compared to the final months of 1994.

Dutch contacts with the members of the Srebrenica Presidency were far from easy. The Dutch were blamed for the perceived failure of the UN to do enough for the people of Srebrenica. Matters were not helped by the character and behaviour of the dominant personalities in the enclave. Naser Orić, the overall military commander, and his two main 'brigade' commanders, Zulfo Tursunović (281 Bde) and Hakija Meholjić, appeared to the Dutch to be little more than gangsters, who terrorized the refugee population and profited greatly from the war. These men jealously protected their own fiefdoms. As the refugees were not represented in the local government, international aid agencies suggested in the second half of 1993 that the refugees should elect their own representative to assist in the distribution of food. The man was found murdered the day after his election.

Orić and his cronies were also responsible for much of the trouble with the Serbs, which stemmed from Muslim raids on Serb communities just outside the enclave. Also, Orić's men had the disconcerting habit of taking up positions close to the Dutch and then opening fire on the Serbs, hoping to entice them and the Dutch into a firefight. At times, when the Presidency found the Dutch insufficiently accommodating at supplying them with desired items, they would turn off the water supply to the Dutch compounds. Local commanders would stop Dutch patrols when it suited them. The Dutch were not at all impressed by the behaviour of the Bosnian Army, and many of the Dutch soldiers had little sympathy for the Muslims. Most shared the judgement of General Nicolai's predecessor, Dutch General Jan Willem Brinkman, that the Bosnian conflict was 'not a matter of good guys against bad guys'.[13]

During 1995, the situation for Dutchbat III deteriorated dramatically. The Serbs began systematically to undermine its operational capabilities. The 13th battalion of the airmobile brigade had relieved the 12th battalion without problems in January 1995. From the middle of February, however, the Serbs started to interfere with Dutch supply convoys. The weekly delivery of fresh and frozen foods ceased to arrive. For a time, hot dinners consisted of rice with varieties of Indonesian peanut sauce. From the beginning of March, the situation appeared to restabilize, but in May the food supply again became erratic. The Dutch soldiers began to live mainly on combat rations.

The fuel situation had always been dire. On 18 February 1995 the last convoy of diesel fuel was allowed in. To be fully operational, the battalion needed 7,000 to 8,000 litres per day. Even in January and February, the battalion had tried to conserve stocks by using only 3,500 litres per day. From 27 March, the Dutch 'minimized' further and brought consumption down to between 800 and 1,000 litres per day. For a while, the battalion secretly used up UNHCR emergency supplies, but there came an end to that too. From 11 May, they were ordered to 'superminimize'. Warrant Officer Both wrote to his wife:

All lights out. There is really a crisis in the [Potočari] compound. Think of it, all the extras, like TV, light, warm water: nothing. No normal meals.

But he added:

What is funny, though: the whole compound is going to have a supermaximize barbecue. The eleven tons of meat which we had sent back because we can't keep it since the freezers will be turned off, did not get past the first [Serb] checkpoint . . . Now we are going to eat it ourselves.[14]

The Muslims received much of what the Dutch could not finish. The pork, though, was offered to the Serbs – and to deliver it in Bratunac they gave Both five litres of diesel for free. Only once, on 20 June, did some more fuel arrive – a pitiful 12,000 litres that lasted fewer than six days.

Without fresh food, the health of the Dutchbat soldiers became an issue. In early June, one of the battalion doctors sent an alarmist letter – leaked to the press – to the 'crisis centre' in The Hague. He feared that the lack of vitamins from fresh food could cause infections and massive health problems with which his staff would not be able to cope.

Such messages added to the worries on the home front. Relatives of the soldiers, who had been organized (with the help of the Ministry of Defence) into support groups, were following the situation in Srebrenica very closely. It did not take much for them to complain about the conditions their boys and girls had to suffer. In January, for example, a concerned father phoned the 'crisis centre' to protest after he had received a letter from his daughter saying that she could not have showers. On a 'quiet day', the centre would receive between 150 and 200 phone calls. During the week in which seventy Dutch soldiers had been held by the Serbs, in November–December 1994, some 3,000 calls came in each day.[15] These relatives turned into an increasingly vocal pressure group. They wanted their boys and girls to come home.

During May, most leave convoys were denied passage through Serb-held territory. Some did get out, but they revealed a disturbing trend: on balance, more soldiers were leaving the enclave than returned. The strength of the battalion diminished. By the beginning of July, the net loss was more than 180 soldiers. Bravo Company alone lost forty-five men, or a third of its manpower.

Morale, which had been decreasing steadily almost from the beginning, now began to hit new lows. The primitive living conditions, the uncertainty of leave, no more mail coming in from home, were completely new and unusual experiences for many soldiers. They felt abandoned by their government and began to wonder what they were doing in Srebrenica. The prospects of adventure and extra pay that had motivated many to sign up for duty in Bosnia began to wear off in the face of the hardship and the loss of faith in their mission. Although UNPROFOR and the majority of Dutchbat officers did not judge the situation dire enough to warrant threatening the Serbs with force to get the convoys through, let alone considering an emergency evacuation,[16] the perception among the rank and file was different. They felt Dutchbat should get out.

Toward the end of May tensions with the Serbs rose. They demanded free access along the road in front of OP Echo in the south-eastern corner of the enclave. They began to intimidate the Dutch by firing close to the observation post. On 3 June, forty Serb soldiers approached the OP and demanded that the Dutch withdraw. When the ten soldiers failed to comply quickly enough, the Serbs opened fire. The OP was abandoned.

On 5 June, two days after the loss of OP Echo, Lieutenant-Colonel Karremans sent a long letter giving his evaluation of the situation, in Dutch, to The Hague. He did not expect 'a large-scale offensive' against the enclave because the Bosnian Serbs lacked the manpower. But he was worried about the situation. The civilian population was in bad shape. UN humanitarian convoys were no longer reaching the enclave. The Serbs had also cut off the smuggling routes to Žepa. The battalion was short on medical supplies. Heavy rainfall had washed away many crops from the fields as well as the improvised power generators in the rivers. The drinking-water supply was no longer functioning, because the system had become blocked. Regarding the men and women of Dutchbat, he wrote that they were completely cut off from the rest of the world and felt like hostages. The lack of supplies meant that the battalion 'as things stand, will be confronted with an emergency situation similar to the one the civilian population has experienced for some time'.

He concluded:

> The circumstances on the southern flank of the enclave as well as the condition of the population and the battalion, both at the operational and humanitarian levels, are becoming so serious that the battalion on the one hand, and the civil and military authorities on the other, are no longer able to turn around the critical situation ... It is now up to the higher echelons to create the parameters which will enable the infantry battalion in the enclave of Srebrenica to carry out, in full, its assigned tasks.

Warrant Officer Both's letters in June reflected the increasing exasperation in the battalion:

> *9 June*: At the end of six months, I ask myself the question what was the point of our presence? I have no answer.
> *10 June*: We all feel the same. A great lack of understanding at the higher levels. We are being forgotten.
> *11 June*: The Muslims are provoking the fighting. 'Get out of here as quickly as possible,' the lads are saying. The people in The Hague don't know what's happening here.
> *24 June*: We talk a lot about the situation to each other. We are of the opinion that we cannot stay here any longer.
> *26 June*: Call the newspapers and tell them we must come home.[17]

In The Hague, Defence Minister Voorhoeve had reached the same conclusion. He wanted to relieve the battalion as quickly as possible. For months he had already been looking, increasingly desperately, for another country to take over the protection of the enclave. On 26 June 1995, in the nick of time it seemed, an agreement was concluded with Ukraine (which already had one company each in Žepa and Goražde) to take over from the middle of July. But the Dutch were so preoccupied with the rotation of Dutchbat that they had failed to recognize the signs that the war in Bosnia was changing inexorably during the Summer of 1995 and that with each passing day a Serb offensive against the Srebrenica enclave was growing more likely.

NOTES

1. Drea Berghorst, ' "Een eervolle, niet eenvoudige, maar uitvoerbare opdracht", De uitzending van Dutchbat naar Srebrenica' (' "An honourable, difficult, but do-able task": The deployment of Dutchbat in Srebrenica'), *Atlantisch Perspectief*, Vol. 20 (1996), p. 10.

2. Jan van der Meulen, 'Hoge verwachting van nieuwe krijgsmacht' ('High expectations for new armed forces'), *Maatschappij & Krijgsmacht*, Vol. 15, No. 1 (February 1993), p. 2.

3. Interview with Mient-Jan Faber by Alex de Meijer, ' "Een houding van niets doen, niet interveniëren, deugt van geen kant" ' (' "Doing nothing, not intervening, is no good at all" '), *Transit*, No. 2 (March/April 1996), p. 21.

4. J. J. C. Voorhoeve and M. van den Doel, 'Nederland moet het initiatief nemen tot actie in Bosnië' ('The Netherlands should take initiative to act in Bosnia'), *De Volkskrant*, 5 August 1992.

5. Berghorst, ' "Een eervolle, niet eenvoudige, maar uitvoerbare opdracht" ', p. 10.

6. Berghorst, ' "Een eervolle, niet eenvoudige, maar uitvoerbare opdracht" ', p. 12.

7. H. A. Couzy, *Mijn jaren als bevelhebber* (*My Years as Commander*) (Amsterdam: Veen, 1996), p. 140.

8. Wio Joustra, 'Kooijmans kiest voor voorzichtigheid' ('Kooijmans opts for caution'), *De Volkskrant*, 11 February 1994.

9. Coen van Zwol, 'Generaal op inspectie bij gijzelaars in Bosnië' ('General inspects hostages in Bosnia'), *NCR/Handelsblad*, 3 December 1994.

10. Herman Veenhof, *Srebrenica, Oorlogsdagboek van Piet Hein Both* (*Srebrenica: War Diary of Piet Hein Both*) (Barneveld: De Vuurbaak, 1995), p. 25.

11. Veenhof, *Srebrenica: Oorlogsdagboek*, p. 75.

12. *Dutchbat in vredesnaam*, p. 161.

13. *De Volkskrant*, 4 March 1995.

14. Veenhof, *Srebrenica: Oorlogsdagboek*, p. 81.

15. Hella Rottenberg, 'De bunker van Voorhoeve' ('Voorhoeve's bunker'), *De Volkskrant*, 6 May 1995.

16. Major Franken allegedly laughed off complaints, saying that soldiers did not suffer from scurvy yet: Henk van Ess and Cees van der Laan, 'Hospikken en houwdegens verdragen elkaar niet best' ('Medics and warriors do not get on'), *Noord-Hollands Dagblad*, 1 September 1995. UNPROFOR had been planning at least since December 1994 to get emergency relief supplies to Srebrenica.

17. Veenhof, *Srebrenica: Oorlogsdagboek*, pp. 89, 90, 93 and 94.

Part Three

Countdown to Massacre

CHAPTER SEVEN

'Breaking the Machine':
The Search for a New UNPROFOR Strategy

During the first weekend in March 1995, top Serbian political and military leaders from Pale and Belgrade met in a ski resort on the slopes of Mount Jahorina near Pale. They were convening to decide on a momentous issue. On 1 January a cessation of hostilities agreement, brokered by former US President Jimmy Carter and UN Special Representative Yasushi Akashi, had come into effect. It would expire on 1 May and the question was, what should the Serbs do once it did? There were clear signs that the Bosnians and Croats saw the agreement as an expedient pause to prepare for another round of fighting. After extensive debate and the consumption of copious amounts of alcohol, a decision was reached. The Serbs would resume fighting as well. They would launch a final campaign in an attempt to force their Bosnian and Croat opponents to settle the war before the year was out. Top of the list in the military campaign plan was the finishing off of the eastern Bosnian enclaves, particularly Srebrenica.

On Sunday 5 March, the British commander of UNPROFOR in Bosnia-Herzegovina, Lieutenant-General Rupert Smith, was invited for a meeting with the (hung over) Bosnian Serb military leadership. Smith, who had assumed his command in Bosnia at the end of January, was meeting General Mladić for the second time. To open the meeting Mladić went through a list of minor complaints. But Smith could detect behind the details a looming concern on the part of the Serbs about the way events were unfolding on a grander, strategic level. The Serbs clearly expected that the Croats and Bosnians would resume hostilities soon. They were particularly concerned with a recent Croat demand that the 12,000 UN troops based in the Serb-held areas of Croatia should be withdrawn. According to an internal UN report, Mladić told Smith that if that were to happen, 'the Bosnian Serbs would demand the UN withdraw from all enclaves in Bosnia, including Sarajevo'.[1]

Mladić had already started to turn the thumbscrews on the UN in the enclaves. Indeed, one of the main items on Smith's agenda was to clear up the problem of recent Serb refusals to allow UN convoys to Srebrenica. The Bosnian Serb commander had justified applying his own 'sanctions' against the safe area as a legitimate response to UN sanctions against the Bosnian Serbs. (In fact, Mladić did allow a road convoy with food through that same day.)

The increased pressure the Serbs were putting on UNPROFOR came as no surprise to Smith. He had come to realize that a resumption of hostilities was likely and that a growing number of incidents and difficulties would pave the way. The challenge he sought to meet in spring 1995 was to devise a strategy for UNPROFOR that ensured that the peacekeeping mission could continue and would not collapse under the strain of a fourth year of war in Bosnia. But Smith failed to convince his political superiors in time, before the fall of Srebrenica, that he had an answer to UNPROFOR's problems and, perhaps, to those of the safe areas.

Lieutenant-General Smith was well-qualified to develop a new strategy. He was arguably the best prepared of all the UNPROFOR commanders. Fifty-one years old, tough, good-looking and trained in the Parachute Regiment, he had already been concentrating on the British operations in Bosnia on a daily basis for over a year, when he worked as assistant chief of the defence staff (Operations and Plans) at the Ministry of Defence in London. Before that, when he was Deputy Commandant of the Army Staff College in Camberley, Smith had been involved in the training of officers for peacekeeping operations. Known as an 'intellectual' soldier, his former commanding officer in the 1991 Gulf War – where Smith commanded the 1st Armoured Division – had given this glowing testimonial:

> Possessed of an exceptionally logical mind and most professional to do business with, he was also refreshingly unorthodox in his ideas and liable to seek less-than-obvious solutions to the problems which confronted him.[2]

These skills were to be tested to their utmost in Bosnia.

When Rupert Smith arrived in Bosnia on 27 January 1995, the cessation of hostilities agreement appeared to be working. The humanitarian convoys were moving, Sarajevo airport was open and, except for the area around Bihać, there was little fighting. But from mid-February the situation began to deteriorate. The Muslims began to mobilize soldiers at a rapid rate, and it seemed clear that they were planning for future offensives. The Serbs then restricted access for convoys, particularly to the eastern enclaves. On 19 March, the Muslims made their move and launched a major offensive from Tuzla into the Majevica hills. Also, in Croatia, President Franjo Tudjman continued to refuse to extend the period of the mandate for the UN troops in his country. It was scheduled to expire on 31 March. The flare up of the war in Croatia which might result would certainly spill over into Bosnia. Indeed, the first signs were already appearing. The activity in and around Bihać seemed to indicate that the Croats were trying to get behind the Croatian Serbs through the Livno valley in Bosnia.

Clearly, the ground was shifting underneath UNPROFOR's feet and the entire peacekeeping operation needed a new strategy to respond to this instability. Smith had tried, immediately after his arrival in Bosnia, to encourage his international staff to think more conceptually. Among the UN military there was an understandable tendency to concentrate on day-to-day operations and on resolving the immediate difficulties that sprang up every minute of every hour. There seemed to be little concern over the medium- and long-term goals that the operation might achieve and the steps that were required to get there. Such matters had always been left to the UN headquarters in New York. But Smith wanted his staff to think through for themselves why UNPROFOR was in Bosnia and how it could best achieve its objectives. He told them: 'we haven't defined the strategic goal'.

In his daily 18.00 briefings, Smith tried to coach his staff. He offered them an imaginative and intricate metaphor to describe UNPROFOR's predicament. UNPROFOR, he said, was like a chain-gang which had to cross a river on whose other bank lay their ultimate objective, peace. In the river, there were a number of stones sticking out of the water. In order to get to the other side, they had to coordinate carefully their each and every step, jumping collectively from stone to stone. However, depending on the intensity of the war, the water level would rise or fall and fewer or more stepping stones would appear. UNPROFOR needed continually to adjust and adapt to the circumstances. To best do that, it would need to know which stepping stones could be seen sticking out of the water and which ones were lurking just below the surface, and, as reliably as possible, it needed to predict the waterflow. The two stepping stones that were vital, in Smith's eyes, were the security of his forces and freedom of movement. Without these 'enabling activities', UNPROFOR could not begin to achieve its most fundamental task: the delivery of humanitarian aid.

Smith quickly gave up on educating his odd assortment of staff officers from all over the world. Conceptual thinking about what, to many, appeared to be an intrinsically flawed UN operation was not only difficult but also seemed of dubious value. None the less, with the aid of some of his staff at UNPROFOR headquarters in Sarajevo, Smith started developing what came to be called 'the thesis': a prediction of the shape of the military campaign in the year to come.

It was clear that the sanctions imposed by the United Nations on the Serbs were hurting. Their economy had suffered greatly and bad economic conditions were sapping the willpower of the Serbian people to continue the war. The armed forces were suffering too, particularly in terms of getting fuel supplies and other raw materials into the country. Also, the Bosnian Serb Army was stretched too thinly. They had a numbers problem, which was getting progressively worse. The Muslims, who as the majority population in Bosnia had always had more mobilizable manpower, were slowly making up for two of their main deficiencies, training and organization.

In February 1995 the Americans secretly had communications equipment flown into Tuzla which would enable the Bosnian Army to coordinate offensive operations between larger units. Although the Bosnian Army still lacked heavy weapons, the Majevica hills offensive in March was an indication of its growing ability to launch larger-scale coordinated offensives. By attacking the Bosnian Serbs simultaneously on multiple fronts, they could make them bleed and, over time, make them bleed to death. However, the Bosnian Army could not yet win a decisive victory by itself. So, in the short term, it would continue to try to get the UN or NATO involved on its side. Neither prospect was a good one for the Serbs.

In short, time was running out for the Serbs. In the estimation of Smith and his staff, the Serbs would have to fight that year in an attempt, if not to conclude the conflict, at least to improve their defensive positions and reduce their vulnerabilities. Improving their defensive positions would almost inevitably mean doing something about the eastern Muslim enclaves. By 1995, the Muslims had built up significant forces within them which posed a clear threat to the Serb lines of communication and rear areas. The Muslims used lightning strikes to tie up Serb troops that were badly needed in other areas.

Neutralizing the enclaves would most likely be a gradual process. By threatening and squeezing them at first, the Bosnian Serbs would put pressure on the United Nations either to have the UN take the demilitarization of the Muslims seriously, or to force the UN to leave the enclaves and allow the Bosnian Serbs to deal with the problem of the Bosnian fighters themselves. Smith's 'thesis' also predicted that the Bosnian Serbs would increase the pressure on Sarajevo in an attempt to force the international community to take a more active interest in brokering a diplomatic solution to the conflict.

In Sarajevo, the UNPROFOR officers were continually testing 'the thesis' against events. Indication after indication appeared to confirm that Smith's predictions were basically right. But how was UNPROFOR to respond? The basic role of UNPROFOR was to help the delivery of humanitarian aid and to contain the effects of the conflict. These roles were founded on the twin principles of impartiality and reliance on the 'cooperation and consent' of the warring parties. On the face of it, a resumption of all-out war would end this cooperation and consent and make UNPROFOR's job impossible.

Since Smith expected trouble in the enclaves, he requested guidance from the UN in New York on the UN policy position on safe areas. As it stood, it seemed clear that the safe-areas mandate was untenable. The UN forces within them were acting as a shield for the Bosnian Army and, at the same time, were hostages to the Bosnian Serbs. Since the UN forces in the enclaves were not strong enough to defend themselves, there had existed an understanding from the beginning that they would have to rely on air power to deter attacks. So Smith also requested clear guidance on the use of air power.

But the UN in New York was not able to provide useful advice on either count. All that the Secretariat and the Department of Peacekeeping Operations possessed in terms of guidance were the mandates provided by the numerous Security Council Resolutions. In response to queries from the field, the UN Secretariat would invariably send a dossier stuffed full with the resolutions. It never provided an authoritative interpretation because that would infringe on the role of the Security Council. It was up to the Council alone to provide clarification. But the Council was extremely reluctant to do this given that its resolutions – particularly the 1993 safe-areas resolutions – were already the result of tortuous compromise and often ulterior motives.

Specifically, on the matter of air power, the problem was that the use of this weapon could draw UNPROFOR into the war as a fully fledged combatant. It was easy to envisage a situation in which an air attack was interpreted by the party at the receiving end as an act of war, rather than as a carefully targeted operation meant to punish a particular transgression. Becoming a party to the war was something all the countries contributing troops to UNPROFOR wanted to avoid. They had therefore designed a cumbersome command structure which decided under what circumstances air power could be used. It carefully evaluated at every stage of the process whether air power was in fact the correct response. It involved a long chain of military commanders in Bosnia, and in Zagreb, the approval of the commander of the UN forces in the former Yugoslavia and the UN Secretary-General's Special Representative, Yasushi Akashi. Finally, NATO, which supplied the aircraft, had also to give its approval. The chain of command was staffed by officers from many countries, each undoubtedly sensitive to the individual concerns of their respective national governments.

To make doubly sure that no action would be undertaken that was against the interests of the international community as a whole, the UN official Akashi (who had overseen the successful UN operation in Cambodia) was specifically chosen for this role. Cautious by nature and highly experienced in the difficult art of UN diplomacy, Akashi was ever mindful of the importance of compromise. If the question was whether or not to use air power, the search for compromise would more often than not dictate not to strike. In an attempt to subject its use to some rational form of control, Akashi had proposed that air power not be employed 'in pursuit of political goals'. He thus hoped to reduce the chances of misunderstanding and of a situation spiralling out of control. This did not work, because *any* use of air power could be ultimately construed as 'political'. In the few cases where the use of air power could not be avoided, Akashi insisted on giving advance warning to the party about to be bombed. This reduced the dangers of misunderstanding and collateral damage, but it did not enhance the air attacks' effectiveness.

What is more, important people within the bureaucracy of the UN in New York had become disillusioned with air power. In November 1994, air attacks were launched against the Bosnian Serbs, who despite repeated warnings and undertakings to the contrary, had continued their incursions into the western Bosnian enclave of Bihać. The Bosnian Serbs had immediately retaliated by detaining several hundred UN personnel. This exposure of the glaring vulnerability of their soldiers in Bosnia did nothing to reassure the UN troop contributors about the usefulness of air power.

Equally worrying were the technical limitations that the air attacks suffered from. It proved to be very difficult, as a December 1994 report by the UN Secretary-General to the Security Council stated, 'to identify suitable targets for possible air action'. The mobility of the heavy guns that the Serbs used to fire into the safe areas, the terrain and the weather all conspired to make the weapons difficult to detect. The fact that UN personnel on the ground were restricted in their movements and could not assist in identifying targets did not help either. And even worse, the Bosnian Serbs were deploying an increasing number of surface-to-air missile batteries in and around Bosnia. Any ground-support mission from the air was likely to have to deal with this threat as well. Indeed, in the Bihać operation NATO aircraft had destroyed Serb missile radars which had locked on to them in preparation for a possible anti-aircraft missile launch. The Secretary-General's report concluded, 'air power is, at best, of very limited utility in compelling the Bosnian Serbs to respect the safe areas'. This boded ill for the enclaves in eastern Bosnia.

★

None the less, in the spring of 1995, UNPROFOR did work hard to overcome the problems of using air power. The idea, associated with Smith's predecessor, Lieutenant-General Sir Michael Rose, of limiting air attacks to 'smoking guns' had not worked very well. It was too difficult to pinpoint a small, in all likelihood mobile, target on the ground and to hit it with precision using fast-flying jet aircraft. Against heavy artillery there was some chance of success, but against mortars and low-calibre guns barely any. Accuracy could be improved by making lower passes over the targets and destroying them with missiles, rather than bombs, but this greatly worried NATO commanders because of the increased vulnerability to Serb air defences. Certain circumstances might warrant a more substantial response with air strikes against fixed targets, such as ammunition depots and anti-aircraft defence systems, which aircraft could hit and destroy with a great degree of certainty. But attacking such targets entailed the risk of rapid escalation and inadvertently changing the local balance of power between the warring parties – something which the victimized party would be likely to perceive as an act of war. Also, such air strikes exposed UN personnel in vulnerable positions on the ground to the risk of hostage-taking or worse.

In one telling example of the problems of UNPROFOR, a Serb 20mm gun that continually harassed humanitarian convoys along the Mount Igman road into Sarajevo could not be destroyed because UNPROFOR and NATO could not devise an accurate and pro-portional response. Air power seemed too disproportionate and too uncertain a means to use and UNPROFOR lacked the required mix of weapons on the ground to take out just the 20mm gun. The gun was not destroyed and continued to hold up convoys. The use of air power remained an unsolvable problem.

The existing capabilities of UNPROFOR, in combination with the too-impractical threat of air power, thus failed to provide an effective answer to the problems it faced. UNPROFOR could not execute its mandate. In particular, it could not achieve the freedom of movement necessary for delivering humanitarian aid, because it could not match, or just exceed, the level of force that was used against it. What UNPROFOR needed was a broader range of weaponry.

The problem was how to achieve this capability. How could

UNPROFOR convince governments which had deliberately sent lightly armed peacekeepers to Bosnia that something much closer to a normal army, as well as more pro-active involvement, were now necessary? Rupert Smith hoped that logic and the strength of his arguments would do the job. However, whenever he presented his 'thesis' to governments and the official delegations that visited him, he tended to be perceived as a scaremonger and excessive pessimist. His analysis seemed too catastrophic to be believable, let alone palatable. Many responded by reasserting their blanket faith in air power. Smith decided to test that faith. Either the international community would allow him, under the right circumstances, to bomb targets other than 'smoking guns' and 'escalate to success', or, if they were not prepared to do so, 'the machine would break'. In the latter case, air power would lose its deterrent effect on the Serbs and, if the international community wanted UNPROFOR to continue to function, it would be forced to create another, better machine with a broader range of capabilities and more secure bases for the UN troops in Bosnia.

UNPROFOR could not go on as it was. 'Muddling through' was no longer an option in the absence of an effective cessation of hostilities agreement. Alternatives began to emerge in the UN and in the military of the troop-contributing countries until there were four choices: a) a withdrawal of UNPROFOR; b) a full-scale military intervention; c) a changed mandate that permitted a greater use of force; and d) a revised mandate that allowed UNPROFOR to concentrate on a more limited number of tasks. The first two were rejected – full-scale intervention was especially firmly rejected because the danger of becoming stuck in a quagmire of interminable, full-scale war was too horrible to contemplate. As for withdrawal, so much had been invested in UNPROFOR over the years that this would mean an unacceptable admission of failure. Public opinion, it was widely believed, would not stand for it except as a last resort. So, this left a choice between options c) and d). Either way, UNPROFOR had to become a tougher and more robust force.

Important people in the UN Department of Peacekeeping Operations in New York had already favoured a tougher UNPROFOR for a while. A confidential internal memo, on 6 December 1994, to the Under-Secretary-General Kofi Annan, eloquently put this group's case:

> UNPROFOR is, in many areas, unable to supply itself, unable to protect the delivery of humanitarian aid, unable to deter attacks, unable to fight for itself and unable to withdraw. All it has going for it are the undoubted dedication and professionalism of its personnel and the determined perseverance of its leadership. But of all the unpalatable options available to it at present, the one with the greatest risk of disaster – . . . the assertive delivery of supplies to UNPROFOR and to civilians in the safe areas – seems the only one that, in my view, carries the slightest hope of breaking out of the present stalemate. If implemented progressively and credibly, it could transform the functioning of the Force and restore credit to the United Nations' often unjustly maligned record in Bosnia and Herzegovina.

Indeed, this may have been the most credible option, but governments still hesitated. Nervous about the vulnerability of their troops in Bosnia and the risk of ending up at war with the Serbs, they could not make up their minds.

In the second week of May, UN Secretary-General Boutros-Ghali called a meeting in Paris of top UN officials involved with the former Yugoslavia. He had been asked by the Security Council to prepare a report in which he outlined the options for UNPROFOR and he needed advice. The meeting was at least partially a result of an incident that had happened earlier in the week. On 7 May, a Bosnian Serb mortar attack on Butmir near Sarajevo had killed ten Muslim soldiers and civilians and wounded thirty. Shelling, by both Muslims and Serbs, had increased the next day and reached the heaviest level Sarajevo had experienced since February 1994. General Rupert Smith had called for air strikes against the Serbs because their shelling seriously violated the heavy-weapons exclusion zone around the city. But both Akashi and Smith's military superior, General Bernard Janvier, opposed him. They felt Smith's proposal to bomb targets other than 'smoking guns' was too escalatory. All the same, the request was passed on to the highest levels, but when it reached Boutros-Ghali in Moscow, he decided to turn it down as well on the advice of his negotiator Thorvald Stoltenberg. However – and this was a first sign that Smith was beginning to convince some people, and in any case at least his own government – British Foreign Secretary Douglas Hurd wrote a letter to Boutros-Ghali protesting against the decision.

This letter reached Boutros-Ghali on 12 May, when he was in Paris meeting Stoltenberg, Akashi, Janvier and Smith. It greatly annoyed the Secretary-General for two reasons. First, he already faced constant harping from the United States in the Security Council about the UN's reticence in using air power. Now he feared that the United Kingdom might join into an unholy alliance forcing him to allow air strikes and thus forcing the UN to become partial in the conflict. Second, Hurd's letter might reinforce the emerging divisions on the issue in the UN hierarchy.

Indeed, although Janvier had been one of those who opposed Smith's request for air strikes four days earlier, he otherwise completely agreed with his fellow general's prognosis for Bosnia. He and Smith predicted to the Secretary-General that there was going to be more fighting in Bosnia, particularly around the eastern safe areas and Sarajevo. UN soldiers might easily be taken hostage – the soldiers in the enclaves were already *de facto* hostages. This would only serve to reinforce the already apparent unwillingness to use air power and to escalate the stakes. In short, Janvier and Smith saw 'no future [for UNPROFOR] as a peacekeeping force while there was no peace to keep'.

Janvier and Smith presented Boutros-Ghali with two stark options. Either UNPROFOR should be allowed to use force or its peacekeeping role needed to be reaffirmed. Clearly, the first option was unacceptable. The second, on the other hand, also had difficult implications. The key to reaffirming UNPROFOR's peacekeeping role would be the introduction of 'measures to enhance UNPROFOR's effectiveness and security'. Effectiveness, at a minimum, meant an ability, if necessary by force, to achieve freedom of movement. Security meant making UN personnel less vulnerable through redeployment. Janvier and Smith proposed concentrating their troops in central Bosnia by withdrawing their most vulnerable personnel from the weapons collection point in Bosnian Serb territory (where Serb heavy weapons that were banned from 'exclusion zones', such as around Sarajevo and Goražde, were kept under UN supervision), and by greatly reducing the UN presence in the safe areas. It was better to have just a few observers and forward air controllers in the enclaves who could call in air power when the safe areas were violated. This kind of presence had at least as much, if not greater, credibility than the 'mini battalions' that were deployed there at that moment. It would counteract the main political weakness affecting the resolve of governments to use force: the vulnerability of UNPROFOR to hostage-taking by the Bosnian Serbs.

The message of his generals was so serious that Boutros-Ghali invited Janvier to come to New York before the end of the month to explain his position, in closed session, to the Security Council and a meeting of the troop-contributing countries.

A week later, on 19 May, Janvier and Smith discussed their ideas at an informal secret meeting of the most senior NATO military personnel – the chiefs of defence staff – in Soesterberg in the Netherlands. It was unanimously agreed that something had to be done. But there was also a sense that the situation was impossible. The generals baulked at the idea of concentrating UNPROFOR in central Bosnia, and they also hesitated at using force to secure freedom of movement.

When they discussed the specific planning initiatives which appeared immediately necessary – the emergency helicopter supply of the eastern enclaves, the creation of a ground corridor to Sarajevo (where some 3,000 French troops risked being cut off) and the expansion of the target list for NATO air attacks beyond just 'smoking guns' and air-defence systems – they came up against the one key truism: that everything hinged on political will. Would their governments be willing to face the difficult political choice of escalation and the inherent risk of sliding into peace enforcement?

When General Janvier briefed the Security Council on 24 May, he caused an immediate political outcry. Janvier had been forewarned over dinner with senior British and French diplomats, the night before his Security Council briefing. The ambassadors told him that his suggestion to redeploy UNPROFOR to central Bosnia would be totally unacceptable to a number of important UN Security Council members, that is, the United States and Germany. Even the French and British governments still had reservations. And indeed, the outcry the next day centred less on the necessity to bite the bullet and consider the use of force than on what was perceived to be Janvier's proposal to 'dump the safe areas'.[3]

In his briefings over the next two days, Janvier was vehemently attacked, particularly by the United States ambassador, Madeleine Albright and the Dutch ambassador, Niek Biegman. Albright told Janvier that while the status quo was untenable and a more effective and robust UNPROFOR required, she could not accept a withdrawal from the safe areas, nor could she accept abandoning the weapons collection points. Biegman equally failed to see how a withdrawal from the enclaves could be contemplated. The mandate, he said, should be strengthened, not reduced. As past experience indicated, only a resolute UN would get its way.

Other ambassadors whose principal worry in fact concerned more robust action rather than redeployment, must have been privately relieved at these reactions. By opposing redeployment, the US and Dutch ambassadors were making more robust action impossible. Albright and Biegman failed to see that the chances of more robust action could only be enhanced if the vulnerability of UNPROFOR to hostage-taking was reduced. By trying to have it both ways, these ambassadors did much to ensure that UNPROFOR remained in its quagmire. It was a fateful mistake, whose effects did not take long to become apparent.

On 22 May, the Bosnian Serbs had forcibly removed two artillery pieces from a UN weapons collection point near Sarajevo. Fighting erupted two days later, just as General Janvier began his briefing in New York. That day there were 2,700 firing incidents. Heavy weapons were being brought in from outside the exclusion zone around Sarajevo and more artillery was being removed from the collection points. On occasion, the Serbs did not even bother wheeling the guns out of the collection points but opened fire from within them. During the evening of 24 May, General Rupert Smith issued an ultimatum that all Serb weapons had to cease firing the next day and that the weapons exclusion zone must be respected. Failure to comply meant that the Serbs would be attacked from the air.

When the Serbs failed to comply in time, NATO did in fact launch an air raid. On 25 May, at 16.20, aircraft bombed two bunkers within an ammunition depot near Pale. It was the first instance of the use of the expanded target list, which NATO had drawn up only that month. In retaliation, the Bosnian Serbs shelled all of the safe areas, except Žepa. In Tuzla, some seventy civilians, mostly teenagers, were killed and over 130 wounded in one mortar attack. When the Bosnian Serbs still refused to comply with Smith's ultimatum, the six remaining bunkers near Pale were bombed the next morning at 10.30. Soon after, and predictably, the Bosnian Serbs began seizing hostages. After a few days, more than 300 UN soldiers were being held. The television pictures of UN personnel chained to potential airstrike targets were beamed across the world.

Smith knew that the Serbs did not know what to do next. They were unlikely to kill the hostages because that would lead to the one response they wanted to avoid: a stiffening of the resolve of the international community to such an extent that a massive military response might be contemplated. If the UN and NATO continued to escalate, Smith believed the Serbs might just be forced to back down and the deterrent effect of the air power saved. But Smith also knew that there was an element of bluff in his threat. The international community might lack the will to escalate to success. In that case, though, the machine would break and force the international community to end the pretence that UNPROFOR was a peacekeeping force.

Indeed, very few were as sanguine as Smith about escalating the stakes. National politicians were too concerned about the domestic backlash that could follow the deaths of the hostages. Even a hardliner like Ambassador Albright, who had applauded the use of air power, changed her tune after the British had made it clear to the Americans that the withdrawal of UNPROFOR had now suddenly become a real option and that the US, in accordance with a pledge it had made as part of an earlier agreed plan, would be called upon to assist in the evacuation with some 25,000 troops. Such an operation was likely to involve serious fighting,[4] and as the Americans were highly anxious about US casualties, this was not an enthralling prospect. So some in the Clinton administration saw the wisdom of the alternative of redeploying UNPROFOR and allowing it to stay. US officials now admitted that there had been a lot of 'wishful thinking that the Serbs would see air strikes as evidence of NATO's strong will'.[5] Although Mrs Albright stopped calling for further air strikes, she still lamely insisted that the UN Secretary General should consider the cost of backing down in the face of the Bosnian Serbs.

On the face of it, the Pale air strikes were a disaster. The international community backed down almost immediately after the Serbs took hostages. Still, there was a glimmer of hope on the horizon, which ultimately paid off – though not in time to save the safe areas. The mood of some important governments, particularly the French and British, was changing. The signs were small and mostly limited to talk, but there were at least a few significant lines written down. In a little-noticed passage at the end of a 'Statement on the Situation in Former Yugoslavia' issued by the North Atlantic Council meeting in a special ministerial session on 30 May, the NATO foreign ministers announced:

> We are ready to support efforts towards the reinforcement of UN Peace Forces in former Yugoslavia, with the aim of reducing their vulnerability and strengthening their capability to act and react.

The British and the French – with the support of the Dutch, who contributed 180 men – offered a 12,000-strong Rapid Reaction Force (RRF) for Bosnia. The speed of the offer, only days after the failed air raids, suggested that it had been in the pipeline and that the waiting had been a matter of finding a good opportunity to make the decision public. In due course, elements of the Rapid Reaction Force would enable UNPROFOR not just to react but to act more robustly.

The dispatch of the RRF did not greatly encourage Janvier, though. He felt a sense of despair. The general was deeply affected by his complete failure to convince the Security Council that a redeployment of UNPROFOR and a strengthening of its mandate were necessary. He felt he had no good reason to believe that the apparent change of heart of his government – under the newly elected, more hawkish, President Jacques Chirac – would give the go-ahead to use the RRF while UNPROFOR remained vulnerable. In the meantime, before it was fully deployed, there was clearly no desire for a rerun of the Pale débâcle. Air power remained unusable. The political will was lacking to make it effective. Since governments gave a political priority to the security of their UN personnel, Janvier had no choice but to make it a military priority as well. On 29 May he sent directive 2/95 to Rupert Smith:

the execution of the mandate is secondary to the security of UN personnel. The intention being to avoid loss of life defending positions for their own sake and unnecessary vulnerability to hostage-taking.

None the less, Smith (with Janvier's backing) refused to give up completely. He wrote in his interpretation of the directive:

Positions that can be reinforced, or it is practical to counterattack to recover, are not to be abandoned. Positions that are isolated in BSA territory and unable to be supported may be abandoned at the Superior Commander's discretion when they are threatened and in his judgement life or lives have or will be lost.

In other words, given the right circumstances, UN units should redeploy to make themselves less vulnerable.

When on 28 May, the Serbs took thirty British soldiers hostage from OPs in the enclave of Goražde, UNPROFOR had urged Dutchbat in Srebrenica to abandon their OPs and withdraw the men to the compounds. But, after consultation with The Hague, battalion commander Karremans refused to do so. He kept his troops in the vulnerable OPs.

By early June, Smith was still looking for ways to make the best of a dire situation throughout Bosnia. Janvier, on the other hand, now considered the situation to be completely hopeless. On 2 June he wrote to Rupert Smith:

We must definitely avoid any action which may degenerate into confrontation, further escalation of tension and [thus] the potential use of air power. This is why I feel your suggestion to use [the] Mount Igman road, even after notification to the Serbs, is untimely in the present circumstances.

This final sentence indicated that Rupert Smith was still pushing for some escalatory move while the Serbs were holding the hostages (the last would be released on 18 June). Smith had proposed not to use air power, but to employ an *ad hoc* battlegroup to open the Mount Igman road into Sarajevo.

The idea was the subject of a meeting between Smith, Janvier and Akashi in the British military headquarters in the Croatian port of Split in the morning of 9 June. This was the last attempt Smith made to come out on top in the face-off with the Bosnian Serbs. But again Janvier rejected Smith's proposal. After Smith presented his case, one of the participants recalled that Janvier responded in 'a tolerant, fatherly way, very quietly, but with absolute conviction and firmness':

> We are a peacekeeping mission. We do not have the option of going to war. We are not authorized to do so. It is not our mandate.

That was the end of the discussion, and Smith accepted the judgement of his superior officer. As during the Butmir incident, he had made his case and he had been overruled. He now agreed with Janvier that 'the mission was dead'.

The party then retired to lunch at a seaside restaurant, a favourite of Akashi's, who always savoured an opportunity to get away from dreary Zagreb. In a lighter mood, the generals spoke about the Rapid Reaction Force. One problem which Janvier raised was whether UNPROFOR could handle the RRF's heavy logistical needs. The generals happily discussed military technicalities.

During the rest of June, Janvier tried to re-establish contacts with the Bosnian Serbs. As one officer put it, he went to them 'as a supplicant'. His immediate priority was to negotiate the release of the hostages, which he achieved by 18 June.[6] Smith meanwhile set to work devising a role for the Rapid Reaction Force. Although it gave him the all-arms capability he had sought (actually it gave him more than he wanted), both he and Janvier doubted that they could ever use it. In a confidential letter of 27 June – published by Leonard Ornstein of the Dutch weekly *Vrij Nederland* – Janvier wrote to Smith:

> we have reduced our exposure and, therefore, our vulnerability to actions by the Bosnian Serbs. On the other hand, we remain vulnerable in many respects to the will of the parties through their actions to restrict and limit our movement, to attack our positions and installations ... We have a right to defend ourselves against such attacks and threats; however, in the absence of a change of political will, we cannot expect the situation to improve significantly in the short to medium term.

The arrival of the Rapid Reaction Force, in Janvier's opinion, would not improve the situation. It could actually create more problems:

> In fact, in some respects its arrival and eventual readiness for operations may raise, in certain quarters, expectations, even demands for more robust action. We will have to be prepared to counter such expectations and demands.

There was thus no option but to let diplomacy have another go:

> This force must not become the vehicle through which we become engaged in peace enforcement. Rather, it should be seen as an additional vehicle for buying time for the peace process to unfold.[7]

The two generals had tried their utmost to convince their political masters that UNPROFOR was in an untenable situation. Although the French and British governments were beginning to show signs of changing their minds, no government had dared to insist on a substantial redeployment to reduce UNPROFOR's vulnerability. And, despite public statements to the contrary, Janvier and Smith had good reason to doubt that any government was willing to sanction the use of force. As a result, air power and UNPROFOR remained paper tigers – and the Bosnian Serbs knew it. They soon took advantage of the weakness of the international community to take Srebrenica.

NOTES

1. Michael Binyon, 'Croatia wooed by Europe as Serbs endorse threat', *The Times*, 7 March 1995.
2. General Sir Peter de la Billière, *Storm Command: A Personal Account of the Gulf War* (London: HarperCollins, 1992), p. 127.
3. Curiously, even some of the chiefs of defence staff had been more concerned about abandoning the enclaves than about using force.
4. NATO had drawn up 'Oplan 40–104' to extract UNPROFOR by putting a massive 60,000-strong force in theatre. Planning quickly revealed, however, that this really had to be a last option, because a withdrawal would almost certainly be a very messy affair and involve heavy fighting. The Muslims, afraid of being left to their fate, would do their utmost to

stop the UN getting out. They would stage incidents – blockading the UN in their bases with women and children, tempting the Serbs to open fire on UN and NATO troops – to get the UN mired in combat. The Serbs, knowing that the UN would be desperate to get out, would try to lay their hands on as much UNPROFOR equipment as possible. A final, unspoken, worry was that the Americans might take the opportunity to attempt to level the playing field in favour of the Muslims with massive air strikes.

5. Stephen Engelberg and Alison Mitchell, 'A seesaw week for US policy in the Balkans', *New York Times*, 5 June 1995.

6. Journalists of the *New York Times* (23 June 1995) and *NRC/Handelsblad* (29 May 1966) have speculated that Janvier struck a secret deal to get the (French) hostages released in exchange for an undertaking that there would be no more air attacks. We have found no evidence of such a deal.

7. Leonard Ornstein, 'Dutchbat wèrd gepiepeld' ('Dutchbat was cheated'), *Vrij Nederland*, 13 July 1996.

CHAPTER EIGHT

'Negotiating with a Mafia Boss':
The Failure of the Frasure–Milošević Talks

A crucial factor leading to the dissolution of Srebrenica was the abrupt rupture on 3 June 1995 of what had seemed a promising political dialogue between the United States and Serbia. That day, the US ambassador to the five-nation Contact Group, Robert Frasure, concluded it was time to break off talks with President Milošević and return to the US. The same contradictory policies that had helped to prevent the introduction of a new strategy for UNPROFOR also torpedoed Frasure's negotiations. The unwillingness of the international community to use force against the Serbs and to accept running risks in the process, meant that only political compromise with the Serbs could save Srebrenica. But Frasure's own government, which had rejected the Smith–Janvier strategy, was also unable to accept the pressing need to compromise with the Serbs – even though it was the only government which could have made a deal stick.

The talks between Serbian President Milošević and Frasure, who was killed in a tragic accident on 19 August 1995 on the Mount Igman road into Sarajevo, had centred on rump-Yugoslavia's (that is, Serbia's and Montenegro's) and Bosnia-Herzegovina's mutual recognition of each other as independent and sovereign states. If this was to be achieved, most of the UN Security Council sanctions against rump-Yugoslavia would be lifted. On 18 May 1995, seven weeks before the fall of Srebrenica, Frasure announced that he and Milošević had reached an agreement. But for reasons that will be explained, the 'Frasure deal' was rejected in Washington. This little-publicized diplomatic initiative had seemed the last good chance for a comprehensive settlement of the war. Now that it was gone, and with the Bosnians, Croats and Serbs all gearing up for a fight, it seemed only a matter of time before the Serbs would move against the eastern enclaves.

★

The five-nation Contact Group had been established in February 1994 in an attempt to unite the Americans, West Europeans and Russians behind a common approach to the conflict in the former Yugoslavia. But a consensus that appeared attractive in theory proved all too difficult to achieve in practice. While the US stumped for the Bosnians, the Russians defended the interests of Serbian President Milošević (as distinct from the Bosnian Serb leader Karadžić) and the Germans supported the Croats. Britain and France, aware that their status as world powers increasingly depended on their permanent membership of the UN Security Council, were essentially pro-UN.

Yet, despite these difficulties, the fragile structure of the Contact Group did manage to sustain itself. In terms of policy there were two important points that helped maintain cohesion. The first was that none of the five countries in the group was prepared to fight a ground war with the Serbs. The second was a tacit understanding that any diplomatic solution to the Bosnian crisis would have to accept some form of territorial (and ethnic) partition.

The international community was not willing to reconquer territory for the Muslims in eastern Bosnia. Even the Vance–Owen plan, which had otherwise been criticized by its detractors as too pro-Serb, had been deemed too ambitious, too pro-Muslim, on this score. Its abandonment had been the start of a process aimed at reaching a more implementable settlement. This would not include any international military intervention. Yet without it, there was no way the Bosnian Army could independently create a permanent and viable territorial connection between central Bosnia and the enclaves.

What this actually meant was that despite the safe-area rhetoric from the Security Council and the frequent beating of war drums by the Bosnian government, the eastern enclaves had little prospect of ever being reintegrated into a Muslim-inhabited hinterland. Privately, the enclaves were widely judged by the key Western governments to be unviable, whether militarily, politically or economically. Srebrenica itself was 'indefensible', as President Izetbegović admitted to a senior UN official on 22 September 1994.

Indeed it seemed that, by 1993, not only the Serbs and the Croats but even the Bosnian government had come to terms with a division of Bosnia-Herzegovina. In a letter of 7 July 1993, Bosnian President Alija Izetbegović told Lord Owen and Thorvald Stoltenberg, who had replaced Cyrus Vance as ICFY Co-Chairman representing the UN, that he himself accepted that Bosnia had been divided. Izetbegović explained that the problem was that the 'stronger and louder element' in Bosnian public opinion was not ready to face the 'unfortunate fact' that partition had taken place on the ground.[1]

During this same period, Haris Silajdžić, the soft-spoken Bosnian Prime Minister who was generally looked upon as one of the few true democrats and multi-ethnicists in the Bosnian leadership, indicated that if the Serbs traded Sarajevo for the enclaves he would be prepared to go to Srebrenica and explain to the people that they had to leave. On 18 November 1993, several months before the US brokered the formation of a Muslim–Croat federation, Lord Owen reported on a remarkable Serb–Muslim rapprochement.

> He [Silajdžić] now talks of the need to have a third of the country, and is quite confident that with a third of the territory, he and Izetbegović could carry a settlement easily through all its stages of acceptance. He is after substantial amounts of territory from the Croats, and Sarajevo from the Serbs. The fact that Karadžić and Silajdžić spent so long together is a start at least. Silajdžić's language has also changed markedly *vis-à-vis* the Serbs. He said that the Muslims had crossed the high psychological barrier of accepting ethnic division – 'the time is right for peace, and the Muslims are keen to make peace with the Serbs.'[2]

During the same round of negotiations, Karadžić was reported to have said that he thought 'the Muslims would now be willing to give up Srebrenica, though not Goražde, in exchange for territory around Sarajevo'. The two men had told the mediators they wanted to continue talks, but outside the public eye, in order to 'prepare a real success'.

The fate of the eastern enclaves also featured prominently in the preparatory negotiations for the creation of a 'peace map' by the Contact Group. During a round of negotiations on 17 and 18 May 1994, the Bosnian Serbs told Contact Group officials that they were prepared to 'trade the Serb-held Sarajevo suburbs of Ilijas and Vogošća for the enclaves'.

On 11 July 1994, Owen and Stoltenberg visited Belgrade in an attempt to influence the Bosnian Serbs via Milošević and the former

Yugoslav President, Dobrica Ćosić. At the meeting, the two Serbian leaders made it clear that they 'attached great importance to resolving the [territorial] question of Sarajevo and raised the question of land swaps involving the eastern enclaves'.

Milošević also told Owen and Stoltenberg that he had been approached by an envoy of Bosnian President Izetbegović. The envoy had said that Izetbegović was ready to discuss a trade-off of the eastern enclaves for Sarajevo, on the condition that Milošević was prepared to recognize Bosnia-Herzegovina.

Though the Bosnian government and Western governments all privately admitted that, ultimately, Srebrenica and Žepa would go to the Serbs, no government was prepared to be seen publicly making territorial deals with the Serbs. After all, would not such a move be perceived as a rewarding of ethnic cleansing and aggression? The dilemma was especially acute for countries where public opinion was strongly anti-Serbian – most pointedly the US, Germany and the Netherlands.

The Clinton administration in particular did not want to be publicly associated with any diplomatic proposal that ceded the enclaves to the Serbs. This became clear during the numerous internal debates between the Contact Group ambassadors. David Ludlow, a British diplomat who represented Lord Owen and Thorvald Stoltenberg, was the Group's secretary. He later wrote a long report to the co-chairmen about the details of the Contact Group negotiations.[3] In his report Ludlow referred to a remark by the US ambassador, Charles Redman, made during a meeting on 19 and 20 May 1994, which crystallized the dilemma many US officials faced:

> In discussion, Redman accepted the possibility of the Žepa and Srebrenica enclaves being swapped for territory elsewhere, such as around Sarajevo. However, he was adamant that the Group could not put forward such a proposal, as they would be faced with public outcry.

It was unthinkable that a territorial swap that involved the enclaves and was mediated by the Group would ever be authorized by the Clinton administration.

Although Redman himself in fact belonged to the 'pragmatic camp' in the Clinton administration, figures such as Vice-President Al Gore and Madeleine Albright opposed any move that appeased, as they saw it, Serbian aggression. Having publicly made a clear distinction between aggressors (the Serbs) and victims (the Bosnians) from the moment they took office, they had stuck to this line ever since. Their credibility would be in doubt and their reputations damaged if they were now to give public approval to a territorial swap involving the eastern enclaves. Albright, moreover, had strongly supported the creation of the safe areas by the Security Council.

Even the more measured Secretary of State Warren Christopher, would not publicly associate himself with a territorial exchange. Though he had for political reasons ditched the Vance–Owen plan in May 1993 and had been among the first to decide that eastern Bosnia was forever lost to the Serbs, publicly he maintained a tough moralistic stance, which he knew best suited the domestic interests of President Clinton. In testimony to the US Senate on 24 February 1994, Christopher emphasized that US policy was *not* intended to be even-handed. The Serbs were the aggressors and the US was not going to impose a solution on the victims.

In order to prevent a breakup of the Contact Group along the obvious fault-lines, its members were forced to stick to the lowest common denominator. It took four months of internal negotiations, as well as numerous consultations with the Serbs, Bosnians and Croats, before the Contact Group was ready to present its initiative in July 1994. The initiative consisted solely of a map. More detailed consti-tutional issues had proved so internally divisive that it was decided to leave them open for the time being. As a result of these internal divisions, all the Contact Group could do was 'serve up yesterday's lunch for breakfast', as UNPROFOR officers privately commented.

The map which was presented to the three warring parties in July 1994 was based on the same 51–49 per cent split as in the 1993 EU Action plan, an earlier failed initiative. The territory under the control of Muslims and Croats was now treated as one entity and fell under the control of the newly established Muslim–Croat federation.[4] Sre-brenica, Žepa and Goražde were allocated to the federation. Two thirds of Sarajevo would come under the control of the federation and one third would remain in the hands of the Serbs.

None of the warring parties liked the proposal. A number of the most sensitive territorial disputes had not been addressed, let alone settled. The Bosnian government nevertheless signed their approval of the map very quickly, fully expecting that the Serbs would not. This way pressure on the international community to take military measures against the Serbs would, the Bosnians hoped, mount rapidly.

On 19 July 1994 the Bosnian Serb leader, Radovan Karadžić, pronounced his view that the map could serve 'in considerable measure, as a basis for further negotiations', but that the Bosnian Serbs could not 'accept' it as it stood, which was what the Contact Group had demanded.[5] On 29 July the Bosnian Serb parliament refused to accept the plan.

The Bosnian Serb refusal caused a rift between the Bosnian Serb politicians and those of Serbia proper. President Milošević, who had hoped that the acceptance of the plan would lead to a lifting of sanctions against rump-Yugoslavia, was extremely irritated by Karadžić's decision. As he made clear on Serbian TV and in the 31 July edition of the Serbian government's mouthpiece *Politika*, Milošević felt that the Bosnian Serbs were forgetting the big picture. They should accept the plan and secure the 'freedom and justice for the Serbian nation' offered by the Contact Group. Crucially, Milošević said that 'accepting the plan does not mean an end to territorial exchanges', explaining that 'all sides have interests in further swaps'.

The Bosnian Serb refusal to accept the map left the Contact Group countries with a difficult problem. They were not prepared to impose a solution by force. The alternative, to win Bosnian Serb acceptance by altering the map, was politically untenable. Unable to solve the dilemma, the Contact Group was thrown into limbo, with its members able to agree on no more than a ban on dialogue with the Bosnian Serbs until they had accepted the map. Well aware that the Contact Group members had no plans for a military intervention, the Bosnian Serbs stayed firm.

The absence of direct talks with the Bosnian Serbs lasted from July 1994 until February 1995, with a brief interruption in December 1994 when the parties agreed to the four-month cessation of hostilities, which began on 1 January 1995. But soon after the ceasefire had come into place, the prospects for peace again deteriorated, with some military activity occurring in late February. The parties issued explicit warnings that if their goals could not be achieved politically, they would switch back to the use of force.

There did seem to be one, at least possible, way out of the political deadlock, which was to respond seriously to President Milošević's standing offer to discuss a recognition of Bosnia-Herzegovina as an independent and sovereign state. In exchange he wanted a lifting of UN sanctions against rump-Yugoslavia and a Bosnian constitution that guaranteed a large degree of autonomy for the Bosnian Serbs. Though these were the main elements, any comprehensive peace package would also inevitably include territorial exchanges, as Milošević was eager to swap the eastern enclaves for Sarajevo.

The recognition of Bosnia-Herzegovina by Milošević was an attractive prospect for the Bosnian government. At a meeting with the Contact Group on 20 April 1995, leading Bosnian politicians Ejup Ganić and Mohamed Šaćirbey promised not to restart the war, once the cessation of hostilities expired, if Serbia and Montenegro were to officially recognize Bosnia-Herzegovina.

With the four-month cessation of hostilities in place, many Western governments, in an excess of relief, had turned away from Bosnia. The sense of urgency faded. And so it was not until March 1995 that the Contact Group launched a serious initiative with Milošević, involving sanctions-lifting and recognition. The negotiations with Milošević were at first conducted principally by British, French and German diplomats. The Germans were involved mainly because they wanted to ensure that a mutual recognition between Bosnia-Herzegovina and rump-Yugoslavia would not set back the chances for mutual Yugoslav–Croatian recognition. Though the successor to Charles Redman as US ambassador to the Contact Group, Deputy Assistant Secretary of State Robert Frasure, took part in the talks, he was forced to keep a low profile. The Clinton administration remained as divided as ever and not yet ready as a whole to associate itself with the talks.

The continuing failure to reach a settlement occurred against the backdrop of a steady escalation of the situation on the ground. The British and French governments, through their military commanders, were well aware of the precarious situation in which the UN troops now found themselves amidst renewed hostilities. Both countries issued explicit warnings to the US that their troops would not spend another winter in Bosnia if by then there was still no settlement. Ironically, the US was as anxious to avoid a fighting withdrawal from Bosnia as the troop-contributing countries themselves, for, as mentioned in the previous chapter, the US had pledged to send in 25,000 combat troops to help get the peacekeepers out.

When the implications of a possible fighting withdrawal dawned on the Clinton administration, a deal with Milošević suddenly became less unattractive. In early May, Robert Frasure received the go-ahead from Washington for serious negotiations with Milošević. Frasure was one of the most experienced diplomats in the US State Department. In June 1991, US President George Bush had awarded him the Presidential Medal for Exceptional Service for his role in precipitating the downfall of the Mengistu regime in Ethiopia and organizing the air-lifting of more than 15,000 Ethiopian Jews to Israel. Frasure had been the US ambassador to Estonia when he was asked to return to Washington and join Richard Holbrooke's Yugoslavia team in July 1994. Almost from the beginning, the sharp-minded Frasure found it difficult to hide his exasperation with the indecision in his own government. Coming out of a US inter-agency meeting on Bosnia he had once commented, 'Boy, that was like a little-league locker-room rally.'[6]

It is no wonder that, as soon as he was given the green light that May, Frasure sat down with Milošević in one of the Serbian president's hunting lodges and worked non-stop on achieving a deal acceptable both to Serbia and the US. Frasure was plied with so much food by the Serbian president that it caused him to remark upon his departure from Belgrade, 'The lambs of Serbia will be delighted that I'm leaving!'[7]

Frasure's last message, which he slipped to Holbrooke during a lunch in Zagreb on 18 August 1995, long after his talks with Milošević had ended and Srebrenica had fallen, indicated that despite his good working relationship with Milošević, Frasure knew when to be tough with the Serbs. He urged Holbrooke to resist the pressure to stop the Croatians from attacking the Serbs in south-western Bosnia: 'This is no time to get squeamish. This is the first time the Serb wave has been reversed. That is essential for us to get stability. So we can negotiate and get out.'[8]

The US decision in May 1995 to talk seriously to Milošević, the traditional villain of the Balkan piece, indicated that in the Clinton administration the wish to end the war was gaining the upper hand over the wish to punish the Serbian aggressors. Back in Washington, Frasure's delicate diplomacy was supported by his direct superior, the flamboyant Assistant Secretary of State Richard Holbrooke.

However, any hopes that Holbrooke may have had that he and Frasure could affect a meaningful shift in US policy were soon frustrated. To Vice-President Gore, Secretary of State Christopher, Ambassador Albright and Leon Fuerth, Gore's representative on the National Security Council, any lifting of sanctions against the Serbs would be anathema. They still believed that the Serbs had to be punished, not wooed. This meant that domestic factors, in Belgrade as well as in Washington, would play a crucial role in determining the outcome of Frasure's negotiations in Belgrade.

On 18 May 1995, after days of intense negotiations, Frasure announced that he and Milošević had reached an agreement. Milošević would recognize Bosnia-Herzegovina and seal off the border between Serbia and Bosnia until the Bosnian Serbs had accepted the Contact Group map. In return, Frasure had persuaded Milošević to accept a suspension rather than a lifting of the economic sanctions imposed by the UN Security Council. Rump-Yugoslavia's assets abroad would stay frozen.

Coming out of a round of talks with Milošević, Frasure gave a description of the man he had been dealing with:

> He's learning very quickly how to be a statesman. Look at him like this: he's a Mafia boss who's gotten tired of doing drugs in the South Bronx and so he's planning on moving to Palm Beach and getting into junk bonds.[9]

Frasure sensed what few others did, namely that for Milošević the time was right to make substantial concessions. He needed a major political breakthrough and he needed it quickly. Both the Croats and the Bosnians had gained in military strength and would soon attack the Croatian and Bosnian Serbs. Milošević wanted to secure through politics the key military gains that the Serbs had made over the past years. Playing into Serbian mythology, he would be able to present himself as the man who had 'won the peace' for the Serbs. This would also allow him to deal once and for all with the Bosnian Serb leader Radovan Karadžić and the nationalist lobby in Serbia proper. (Though Milošević was not prepared to see the Bosnian Serbs getting defeated militarily, he was very keen on preventing Karadžić from becoming the 'King of all Serbs'.)

In the absence of a deal with the United States, however, Milošević would have no choice but to come in on the side of the Bosnian Serbs. The alternative would be political suicide at home. As Serbian Foreign Minister Jovanović publicly warned in the third week of June 1995,

> If a foreign intervention were to massively destroy or drive away the Serbs [in Bosnia], we would no longer be able to put a brake on the solidarity of the people [in Serbia proper] with their brothers [in Bosnia]. Any government that refuses to defend them, would fall.[10]

Milošević had made his move towards peace. The question now was whether Frasure's superiors in Washington would back the agreement. Time was pressing. As Washington weighed the pros and cons, the number of registered 'firing incidents' was increasing rapidly all over Bosnia. Particularly in Sarajevo, more and more people were getting killed. Heavy fighting had erupted near Brčko in the Posavina corridor. In and around Srebrenica the shelling and sniping had also increased. The moment in which the parties would substitute politics with force was approaching fast.

Paris and London nervously awaited the result of deliberations in Washington. The newly elected French president, Jacques Chirac, had warned the US that there was a 'direct link' between a deal between Frasure and Milošević and the continued presence of French troops in Bosnia.

Despite considerable efforts on the part of Frasure and, to a lesser extent, Holbrooke, it soon became clear that the deal in its present form was not going to work. Though Milošević had agreed to this suspension in lieu of a lifting of sanctions, he had in turn imposed the condition that rump-Yugoslavia would be free from sanctions for a whole year and that at the end of that period it would be the UN Secretary-General who would make a recommendation to the Security Council on whether or not to reimpose them. Many in the Clinton administration feared that Russia would veto a reimposition of sanctions once they had been suspended, regardless of whether Milošević behaved badly or not. The President needed an agreement that included a clearly distinguishable punitive element if it was to be sold to the American public. The deal as it stood lacked such an element, which meant that Secretary of State Christopher could not support it. Ambassador Albright reportedly threatened to resign over what she called the 'softly-softly pact' with Milošević.[11]

After much deliberation, Frasure was instructed to return to Milošević and offer a different suspension mechanism. Under the toughened-up US proposal, any single permanent member of the Security Council (in other words the US), could at any given time reimpose the UN sanctions. This could only then be overturned by an affirmative vote of the whole Council. But the same permanent member that had reinstated the sanctions would of course veto that affirmative vote.

Not only was the new US offer unacceptable to Milošević as he told Frasure on 22 May, but it would never have found support among any of the other permanent Security Council members. Unless the 'Serbia-bashers' in the Clinton administration had already privately come to accept the inevitability of a military conquest of the eastern enclaves by the Serbs, theirs was a high-risk approach.

Meanwhile, shells continued to rain down on Sarajevo. Bosnian troops massed around the city in preparation for an (almost certainly futile) attempt to break the siege if the Frasure talks failed. Croatian troops were concentrated around the Krajina, both in Croatia proper and in Croat-held Bosnia. The Serbs, for their part, were trying frantically to widen the northern corridor. They were also digging in to defend the Serb-held Sarajevo suburbs against the Bosnian Army, a task made considerably easier by the fact that the Serbs knew all the details of the Bosnian Army's offensive plans. Finally, situation reports from Dutchbat stated that military activity in and around the Srebrenica enclave was increasing.

The Serbs and UNPROFOR were on a collision course, and the Serbs were at a clear military advantage. If they could not get the Contact Group map changed through politics, then they would do so by force. Frustrated in his attempts to reach a political solution with the US and conscious that the Bosnians and the Croatians would soon attack, Milošević no longer felt the need to restrain the Serb generals in their wish to escalate.

Though Frasure continued his talks on sanctions with Milošević, the two men could not bridge the gap that divided Serbia and the United States. On 3 June a very frustrated Frasure was forced to admit he was getting nowhere. He had in vain tried to get it across to Washington that the dialogue with Milošević on sanctions and recognition was no longer merely a technical matter. The real issue was, as one American diplomat put it: 'How much are we prepared to get rid of the Bosnian tar baby?' Frasure himself pointed out that if the US believed that only Milošević had the power to deliver a settlement, then Washington should be prepared to compromise.

The complication was that Milošević's patience was wearing thin. While the Clinton administration had procrastinated, the pressure on Milošević to abandon the political track and take sides with the generals only increased. Unless the Serbian president could be confident that the US would offer him something serious and *soon*, he would not settle. A few days later Frasure told Lord Owen, who was on his last visit to Belgrade, that he hoped he would be called back to Washington for consultation. Owen remembered Frasure saying that, because of the policy changes of his own administration, his real problems lay in Washington, not in Belgrade.

On 3 June 1995, the day that Frasure and Milošević ended their negotiations, Serb troops overran OP Echo, the most southern of the Dutch observation posts in the Srebrenica enclave. Near Kalesija in the so-called Sapna Thumb, a Dutch armoured vehicle was hit by a shell, resulting in serious injuries to two crew members. The day before, a US F-16 had been shot down. On 1 June, Serb troops had carried out an ambush inside the Srebrenica enclave, killing thirteen civilians. It was clear that Milošević regarded the dialogue with the United States as finished and had stopped restraining Mladić. But for a miracle, the fate of the enclaves in eastern Bosnia seemed fixed to a disastrous course.

Though Owen's successor as EU mediator and Conference Co-Chairman, Carl Bildt, took over the negotiations with Milošević from Frasure, the Serbian president did not take this new round of talks very seriously. He knew that Bildt could not possibly bring round the Clinton administration given Frasure's failure to do so. The power to lift or suspend UN sanctions lay not with a former Swedish prime minister representing the European Union, but with the United States government.

The EU governments, as well as generals Janvier and Smith, did not appear to have quickly grasped how fateful Frasure's failure was. During his last meeting with the EU foreign ministers before stepping down, in Brussels on 29 May, Lord Owen had explicitly warned the Europeans that they should not underestimate the Serbs, as they were 'skilful' and 'serious'. He criticized the phrase in the draft ministerial declaration which mentioned that all six of the safe areas should be protected. As things stood, UNPROFOR would be 'hard-pressed' to do this, and Smith and Janvier were therefore right to argue that UNPROFOR should regroup to central Bosnia. Knowing that what he was saying was irritating the German and Dutch governments, he nevertheless stressed that it was now more important than ever to 'pursue agreement with Milošević on mutual recognition [between rump-Yugoslavia and Bosnia-Herzegovina]'.

Dutch Foreign Minister Hans van Mierlo, who was hoping that Ukraine would soon agree to replace the Dutch troops in Srebrenica with its own, told some of his colleagues that the Dutch government had information that Serb forces were moving in on the Srebrenica enclave, possibly with the intention of taking Dutch hostages. Van Mierlo none the less said that he did not see why a deal with Milošević should be actively pursued and that the ministers should not expect too much from Milošević. He let it be known that the Dutch government also opposed the withdrawal of UN military observers from Serbian-held territory. German Foreign Minister Klaus Kinkel, for his part, argued that Milošević should be urged to recognize not only Bosnia but Croatia too.

Judging from their public statements, the EU governments, particularly French President Jacques Chirac, seemed to entertain high hopes for the Bildt–Milošević talks. Bildt's approach was also fresh. Unlike the Americans, he regularly exchanged information with the military commanders. From the perspective of Janvier and Smith, since air power had become a paper tiger and they had not been allowed to concentrate their troops, the Bildt talks were the only hope of preventing disaster. But they 'did not realize until July', as one UNPROFOR officer explained, 'that Bildt was very much playing second fiddle'. By then a month had passed since the only dialogue that might have prevented disaster, that between the Clinton administration and Milošević, had ended.

On 24 June, General Mladić indicated that the continuing raids by Muslim forces from the Srebrenica enclave in his view constituted a *casus belli*. In a letter to the UNPROFOR headquarters in Sarajevo, Mladić referred to several attacks that had taken place the day before.

These attacks against the territories controlled by R[epublika] S[rpska] Army . . . brutally violate the status of [the] Safe Area of Srebrenica. Due to that fact I strongly protest and warn you that we will not tolerate such cases in future.

Despite the warning, in the early morning of 26 June, Muslim troops commanded by Zulfo Tursunović raided Višnjica, a Serb hamlet five kilometres west of the enclave's perimeter, killing one Serb soldier and wounding three Serb civilians. The Bosnian Serb Army's spokesman, Milovan Milutinović, immediately summoned the international press to the scene. Preparing the ground for the offensive that the Serbs were about to launch, he told the assembled journalists: 'The Muslim soldiers who carried out this attack crossed lines patrolled by Dutch UN troops whose job it is to prevent just this kind of action. We therefore conclude that the UN forces are aligning themselves with the Muslim army.'[12] The Serbs argued that, since the UN peacekeepers had failed to disarm the Bosnian troops in Srebrenica and the latter had continued to raid Serb villages, the safe area no longer *was* a safe area. It was the Serbs' right to go in and 'demilitarize' the area themselves.

NOTES

1. Owen, *Balkan Odyssey*, p. 194.
2. Lord Owen to EU foreign ministers, COREU, 18 November 1993, in Owen, *Balkan Odyssey*, CD-ROM edition (PO Box 9414, London SW1H 9ZA).
3. David Ludlow, 'Direct governmental involvement in the search for a negotiated settlement to the conflict in Bosnia and Herzegovina with special reference to the work of the Contact Group, September 1992–July 1994', in Owen, *Balkan Odyssey*, CD-ROM edition, Reference 190.
4. The Bosnian Croats and Muslims on 1 March signed a US/German-brokered federation agreement. The president of Croatia, Franjo Tudjman, who had never shown much enthusiasm for Croat–Muslim rapproachement, publicly emphasized that he had received serious guarantees from President Clinton and the international community

regarding the resolution of all of Croatia's problems, including the return of Serb-held territory.

5. Owen, *Balkan Odyssey*, p. 285.

6. Roger Cohen, 'Taming the bullies of Bosnia', *New York Times*, 17 December 1995.

7. *New York Times*, 17 December 1995.

8. *New York Times*, 17 December 1995.

9. Misha Glenny, 'Washington will miss skilled envoy whose Bosnia mission was torpedoed', *The Times*, 21 August 1995.

10. ' "Reiner Wahnsinn": Außenminister Vladislav Jovanović über Belgrads Verhältnis zu Karadžić', *Der Spiegel*, No. 23 (1995), p. 140.

11. Dusko Doder and Askold Krushelnycky, 'Albright "stalls" softly-softly pact with Milošević', *The European*, 9 June 1995.

12. Stephen Kinzer, 'Bosnian Muslim troops evade UN force to raid Serb village', *New York Times*, 27 June 1995.

Post Mortem

After the rejection of the Smith–Janvier military strategy and the failure of the Frasure–Milošević negotiations, the Serbs knew that the eastern enclaves were essentially theirs for the taking. Although at the strategic level UNPROFOR had been prepared for a long time, at the tactical level it was still surprised when the attack on Srebrenica actually came. There were a number of reasons. UNPROFOR intelligence officers had long estimated that the Serbs would need a large infantry force to overcome the 3,000 or 4,000 armed defenders of Srebrenica. What they had failed to detect was just such a large-scale troop build-up during June. Indeed, even after the Serb attack had begun, on 6 July, Dutch soldiers detected no sign of a full-scale offensive. No more than four or five tanks or one hundred Serb infantrymen were ever seen advancing at one time. There had also been no sightings of an artillery build-up – another sure sign of offensive intent. The Serbs appeared to open their attack with the same artillery they had had in position for a long time.

Moreover, the Serbs attacked only from one direction and not, as one would have expected with a surrounded safe area, from several at once. Thus UNPROFOR intelligence concluded that the Serbs were seeking to fulfil no more than their long-standing aim of seizing the south-east corner of the enclave and gaining unimpeded control over the important road there. This conclusion was reinforced by Lieutenant-Colonel Karremans. In fact, the Dutchman had acquired a reputation within UNPROFOR of being somewhat alarmist as a result of his repeated complaints about Dutchbat's situation. Under attack, in July, however, he was remarkably restrained in his official reports and played a significant role in (mistakenly) minimizing the sense of danger. The final contributing factor in the misreading of the situation was that many officers and politicians simply could not believe that the Serbs would dare take an area under the protection of the United Nations.

The Serb offensive was well planned and well executed. They achieved total tactical surprise. By striking with limited forces along a front where an attack was already expected, they managed to throw the UN off balance for a number of days. Also, the Serbs, as always, acted with caution. It is clear from the pattern of their moves that, until the moment they set foot in Srebrenica, they did not totally discount a strong international response. Every time NATO air attacks appeared imminent, they would pause, and only when the skies remained empty would they resume their advance. They also very carefully avoided shooting to kill at the blue helmets. After it was all over, Karremans justifiably praised Mladić: 'Militarily, the Dutch battalion was cleverly outmanoeuvred by the Bosnian Serb Army.' It had been, Karremans said, 'almost like a game of Pacman'.

When Lieutenant-Colonel Karremans made this comment on 23 July 1995, he clearly did not yet realize what horrific fate had befallen the men of Srebrenica. And he was not alone in underestimating the savagery of the Bosnian Serbs. Few people had expected them to attempt full-scale annihilation of the men of Srebrenica. Yet it should not have come as a surprise: the portents had been there since the beginning of the conflict.

Radovan Karadžić offered a simple explanation for the Srebrenica massacre: 'It was not a slaughter organized by the army, but revenge attacks by Bosnian Serbs whose relatives had been killed by Muslims earlier in the war.'[1] Yet although hatred for the Srebrenica Muslims must have played a part, the Serbs' actions were not characterized by wild rage. The killings were skilfully prepared for and organized. In addition, the executions do not appear to have been carried out solely or even predominantly by local troops and militias. Erdemović, the Croat from Tuzla, who as a member of the 10th Sabotage Detachment participated in the mass execution near Pilica, was certainly not a local. The soldiers who appear in the 'Petrović video', filmed along the Bratunac–Milići road on the afternoon of Thursday 13 July, wore regular BSA uniforms. Moreover, various witnesses report the presence of paramilitary units, including Arkan's Tigers, and special police forces in the area.

As for General Mladić, he and other top Bosnian Serb Army officers

gave a slightly different explanation from that of Karadžić: The Srebrenica enclave, they claimed, contained 3,000 to 4,000 Muslim soldiers. Many of these men were killed in combat. In reality, whatever
number of Bosnian soldiers there were in the enclave they put up
little resistance and essentially melted away in the face of the advancing
Serbs. The majority appear to have successfully escaped to central
Bosnia. As for the 'soldiers' Mladić spoke of, there were virtually no
signs of combat witnessed by the Dutch soldiers or Muslim women
who travelled along the road where most of these men were captured.
The vast majority of the men were subsequently killed by the
Bosnian Serbs. Almost all of them were civilians. (This is not to
mention the fact that the Bosnian Serbs seem to have captured more
prisoners than, by their own account, there were soldiers in the
enclave.)

All prisoners, according to General Mladić, were screened for 'war
crimes'. But this process was a perfunctory one. Virtually all the captured men, guilty or not, were executed, an act that constituted the
most serious single war crime in Europe since the Second World
War. Executing prisoners of war violates the Geneva Conventions.
Executing civilians not only violates the Geneva Conventions but is
also classified as a 'crime against humanity'. What is more, there seems
little doubt that the Serbs' intention was a genocidal one.

So, if it is not as simple an answer as 'revenge', and if the suggestion
of 'combat casualties' is patently false, why did the Bosnian Serbs kill
the men of Srebrenica in cold blood? Much of it seemed to have to
do with the character of the war in Bosnia. Muslim men posed a
pointed threat to the Serbs, who were educated in the traditions of
people's war and who aimed to create an ethnically pure Serb territory.
And, as the police chief of Serb-controlled Banja Luka commented
in 1992, 'In ethnic warfare the enemy doesn't wear a uniform or carry
a gun. Everyone is the enemy.'[2] Civilians were considered indis-
tinguishable from soldiers. The long-term success of ethnic cleansing
depended on killing off the Muslim men, without whom the population's women and children would have no means of returning to
their birthplaces. And since Srebrenica had been one of the main
refuge places for Muslims from eastern Bosnia, executing the men
would give the Serbs a more secure hold over the region. Both the
requirements of people's war and the dictates of ethnic purity

demanded that potential resistance, now and in the future, be mini-
mised. As many men as possible had to be killed.

The details of the Srebrenica massacre support the contention that
the project of creating an ethnically homogeneous eastern Bosnia was
controlled, without doubt, by the Bosnian Serb military and political
leadership and, most likely, by the rump-Yugoslav military and political leadership as well. The gruesomely efficient implementation of the
massacre indicates high-level support. The fact that it appears likely
that more troops were involved in catching the Muslim men along
the Bratunac–Milići road than in conducting the actual attack on the
enclave only underlines this. The systematic way the captured men
were dealt with also suggests careful preparation: most were transported to one of a number of specific sites before being interrogated
and then shot. One indication that these sites – and the incidents that
took place on them – were not just random lies in a particular recurring
detail. The Muslim survivors from Karakaj near Zvornik mentioned
that they were ordered to take off their shoes before being taken out
to be shot. At another execution site near Nova Kasaba, Dutch soldiers
noticed rows of shoes in a field. Ordering people to take their shoes
off shortly before killing them does not occur as a natural or standard
part of a process, which means that the Serbs were operating according
to instructions. Four years of war must have taught them that stripping
a body of recognizable belongings makes subsequent identification of
the bodies more difficult.[3]

The deportation of the women and children and the capture, detention and execution of the men were parts of an integrally planned
operation. Thus it is particularly damning that from the beginning
General Mladić had taken a personal interest in the Srebrenica operation. He negotiated directly with Karremans about the deportation
of the women and children and the separation of the men. He turned
up in Potočari and announced to one of the Dutch officers that 'it
will be done according to my orders'. A number of the Muslim
survivors of the massacre claim to have seen him as well, mainly at
the interrogation sites, but in one case at an execution site. These
appearances seem to indicate, perhaps not so much that he revelled
in the fate that had befallen the Muslim men, but that he felt it
necessary to stiffen the resolve of those of his men faced with the job
of actually killing the Muslim 'war criminals'.

The evidence for the involvement of the Belgrade leadership in the Srebrenica operation is more circumstantial. US intelligence sources insist that armoured units from the Yugoslav Army wete involved in the attack on the enclave. The tribunal in The Hague has accepted the fact of Yugoslav Army involvement as evidence in the indictment of Karadžić and Mladić. Since the Yugoslav Army participated in all major Bosnian Serb Army offensives, it would have been strange if it had not done so in the case of Srebrenica. Furthermore, the far-reaching integration of the Bosnian Serb Army into the Yugoslav Army and its total logistical reliance on the Yugoslav Army resources are well-documented. Thus, for example, General Djordje Djukić, the man responsible for logistics for the Bosnian Serb Army, carried regular Yugoslav Army identity papers when he was arrested by the Bosnians in January 1996. So, at the very least, the Yugoslav Army leadership must be guilty of collusion with the attack on the Srebrenica safe area. It is more than likely that they participated in the planning for the attack and approved it. Given the scale of the operation and its political repercussions, it is also more than likely that the top political leadership in Belgrade was aware of the operation and con-sented.

Why was Mladić not restrained by the presence of UN peace-keepers? By July 1995, the general seemed on a perpetual high. He had repeatedly humiliated the international community over the course of the war. In the hostage crisis (during which, for a while, he *had* apparently been seriously worried that the UN would escalate its involvement), he had outdone himself. He clearly believed he could not go wrong and that he could get away with anything, including murder. As for Srebrenica, it was an especially attractive target for rubbing the humiliation in even deeper, because of the presence of Dutch peacekeepers. Mladić harboured a particular resentment towards the Dutch, whose successive governments had consistently called for tougher action against the Serbs since the beginning of the war. In a 15 March 1996 interview with the Belgrade weekly *Nin* he said:

> There is no greater shame for us Serbs than to be bombed by some Dutchman. I have no idea whom Holland could bomb on its own. Not even Denmark, but it simply dared to bomb Serbs. Their miserable Van den Broek [Dutch Foreign Minister

and one of the key European Union negotiators at the start of the conflict in 1991] committed great atrocities and made a great contribution to the collapse of former Yugoslavia.[4]

Mladić was out to teach the international community, and the Dutch in particular, a lesson. It was also a signal to the United States that the price of the lost opportunity of the Frasure talks was a high one.

The Muslims, in general, were aware of the fate that awaited them. Their desperate attempt, *en masse*, to break through Bosnian Serb lines from the night of 11–12 July onwards reflected this. Why though, if they knew their likely fate, had they not seriously tried to defend the enclave? Perhaps their greatest weakness was low morale. Naser Orić, the hero of the 1992–3 defence of Srebrenica, had left the enclave in April and had not returned.[5] A majority of the Muslims could not have been unaware, and even President Izetbegović had on occasion privately admitted it, that the enclave was essentially indefensible. The men were poorly armed and, most crucially, lacked heavy weapons – in spite of the US Defense Department's claim that the Bosnians had more mortars than the Bosnian Serbs.[6] The Bosnians had also concentrated on a risky strategy. Rather than fight themselves, they believed their best chance of defending the enclave lay with forcing the UN to intervene on their behalf. The strategy completely failed, as was clear from a last encounter between Dutch Captain Groen and the acting Bosnian commander, Ramiz Bečirević, two hours before the town fell:

> Suddenly Ramiz appeared in the Opsroom, clearly shaken. He wanted to know whether there would be any air attack from the UN. I told him I no longer believed so and that we had to try and evacuate as many civilians as possible. I asked him whether his people could help me, but I did not get through to him. Bewildered, he left the Opsroom a little later.[7]

Clearly, in banking on this strategy, the Bosnians had devised no alternative.

But why did the UN not intervene? The problem of intervention goes back to the creation of the safe areas, which were never meant to be a serious long-term solution, at least in the eyes of NATO countries contributing troops to UNPROFOR. Indeed, all of these countries but for the Canadians (who soon changed their mind) and the Dutch (whose offer was driven by a combination of impractical ideals and a moral superiority complex), refused to offer troops for the eastern enclaves in 1993.[8] At least one of the tragedies for Srebrenica was that while it was fortunate to get troops from one of the few countries that did take the safe-area concept seriously, that country did not have the means, the wherewithal, or finally the will, to make it work.

A second basic problem with the UN operation was that it relied on the cooperation and consent of the interested parties (that is, the Serbs, the Muslims and the Croats) and that it was driven above all things by the desire to remain impartial. There existed a very strong sense, as Yasushi Akashi put it, 'that the man you bomb today is the same man whose cooperation you may require tomorrow for the passage of a humanitarian convoy'.[9] In the specific case of the eastern enclaves, this attitude led to a complete dependency on the goodwill of the Bosnian Serbs to let supplies and manpower through. Very few politicians and soldiers ever questioned this premise of impartiality. Few accepted that one could force an obstreperous party into allowing convoys through and still remain impartial – as long as one was prepared to use force against all parties on grounds deemed legitimate by the international community and founded in international law.

But the fact is that relying on the cooperation and consent of the Bosnian Serbs meant that the eastern safe areas could not work. A common argument is that these safe areas failed because of a lack of troops. The UN Secretary-General had requested 34,000 troops, but he did not even reach the minimum requirement of 7,600. The truth is that no number of troops, except, ironically, for perhaps a very small total, would have worked. The more troops that were put in the enclaves the greater the logistical nightmare would have been. As long as they lacked essential supplies (a condition the Serbs seemed determined to maintain), increasing the number of UN troops would make no difference. Counterintuitively, it is conceivable that a smaller group of soldiers could have protected the enclaves no worse and possibly better. They could have been more easily supplied through the air and, if need be, evacuated by helicopter. But their strength (and this was, in effect, no different for the Dutch) would have had to rely on a credible threat located outside the enclave – which brings one to the question of air power.

Could the enclave have been saved by air power? There were undoubtedly technical complications. As a precision instrument, air power was too blunt for the task of effectively destroying 'smoking guns'. There was always a significant danger of collateral damage and subsequent escalation. Air power was also a cumbersome tool, which could not respond quickly enough to developments on the ground, because of a byzantine and time-consuming command structure. Any number of things could – and in the case of Srebrenica, did – go wrong. But despite these technical shortcomings, the main problem with the use of air power lay in the political arena, which almost universally was characterized by a softly-softly caution (except for some factions in the US government, which had no troops on the ground).

The Bosnian Serbs had a very well controlled and disciplined army. Their operations – and Srebrenica is a prime example – were cautious and methodical. At every stage, they took into account the possibility of a strong UN reaction. Even in their war against the Muslims, they were loath to run risks and suffer casualties. Their victories were won 'on the cheap'. In the case of Srebrenica, what would they have done if they had been threatened with a massive use of NATO air power? They would have probably backed down, at least for a while.

But, as General Janvier correctly recognized in July 1995, there was no *political* will on the part of the troop-contributing countries to escalate. They feared the Bosnian Serbs would again take UN hostages, just as they had done after the Pale raids in May. The military dilemma of whether or not one could escalate to success through the use of air power was a tough one, and many soldiers doubted that one could against the Bosnian Serbs. But without the political will to risk casualties, or another round of hostage-taking, there was no point in even considering air attacks.

General Janvier and General Smith were responsible officers who presented their political masters with some hard, unpalatable truths in the first half of 1995. General Janvier, in particular, has unjustly been much maligned. He is often blamed for losing Srebrenica because he did not authorize massive air strikes. Yet, in July 1995, having been forbidden to withdraw the Dutch 'mini-battalion' from Srebrenica and knowing full well that neither the Dutch government nor any other government was prepared to risk hostages being killed, he found himself in a 'no-win' situation. If he had opted for air strikes, the Serbs would have again taken a large number of hostages and would have tightened their stranglehold on Sarajevo. Instead, Janvier did what was expected of him by the governments of the UNPROFOR troop contributors: he gave a priority to saving the lives of his 'blue helmets'.

The most fundamental dilemma of all, which the international community to its detriment never resolved, was a moral one. How could one combine the moral imperative to alleviate suffering with the moral imperative not to let aggression pay? Was it right to have opposed ethnic cleansing and instituted 'safe areas' in eastern Bosnia, if one was unwilling to put one's life at risk to protect the people in those areas? All of the governments that supported the safe-area resolutions failed to resolve the dilemma, but the Bosnian, US and Dutch governments failed more than others, for it was these three countries that, each in its own way, most directly obstructed an earlier admission of failure that, however unjust the result would have been, might have saved lives that are now lost.

The Bosnian government, for understandable reasons, opposed abandonment of the eastern enclaves throughout the war – even though its own people were desperate to get out. Although the government did accept the idea of a swap of territories with the Bosnian Serbs, it never finalized a deal, because it always believed a better one could be had – until it was too late and Srebrenica and Žepa were lost. The Bosnian government also did their people no favour – although again their motives were understandable – by not demilitarizing the safe areas. This only reinforced the desire of the Bosnian Serbs to take the enclaves and also helped alienate the UN peacekeepers.

The Dutch government did send troops to Srebrenica and was thus prepared to run some risk for the people of Bosnia. But, even at that time, it should have been clear that a Dutch battalion in the eastern enclaves was not a good idea. The government should have realized this in 1993 when no other Western government joined it in committing troops. It then compounded its error by sending so many troops, which served to create a completely false impression of strength and resolve. With a lack of supplies, the Dutch battalion, as Defence Minister Voorhoeve himself admitted, was 'barely operational' by June 1995. A third error of judgement was their opposition to a withdrawal of UNPROFOR units from the eastern enclaves.[10] The final error was that the government continued to talk tough while at the same time widely advertising its search for another country to take over their role in Srebrenica. The Serbs undoubtedly picked up on these contradictory signals and judged – correctly – that the Dutch government would cave in quickly after its troops were attacked and Dutch hostages taken. As with no other country, the Dutch were cruelly caught out and the terrible hollowness of their 'principled course' was exposed.

As for the Clinton administration, it pursued a high moralistic policy for which it was totally unwilling to accept responsibility. It insisted, particularly in the UN, on tougher action against the Serbs, but refused to support it with American ground troops. Even worse, when Generals Smith and Janvier tried to create the preconditions on the ground which, in actual fact, might have made tougher action possible, the US ambassador to the UN strongly opposed their proposal to withdraw UNPROFOR units from the eastern enclaves. Such statements undoubtedly also stiffened the resolve of the Bosnian government to hang on to them, by creating the false hope that the US might fight politically, if not militarily, to prevent the Serbs from obtaining the enclaves at a low price. That was a pipe dream. Other senior figures in the Clinton administration, like Warren Christopher since May 1993, had long given up on the enclaves – even though the US never explicitly made the Bosnian government face this fact.

There is a tendency now to give the US virtually all the credit for the peace agreement that was achieved in Dayton in November 1995. There are even suggestions that the US created the actual circumstances that allowed the agreement to fall into place, after the Europeans had miserably failed for so many years. Yet, the truth is that agreement only became possible after a number of preconditions were met over which the US had some, but certainly not total, control. Essentially, the warring parties had themselves achieved a position on the ground which made them amenable to a peace deal. The Croats conquered the Serb territories within its borders – except for Eastern

Slavonia – in two lightning offensives in May and August. The Muslims, with the indispensable help of the Croats, also conquered some territory in western Bosnia. The artillery of Smith's Rapid Reaction Force finally broke the siege of Sarajevo (after the last British troops had left the safe area of Goražde). It was the combined effect of these military actions that made the Serbs willing to accept peace.[11]

But the United States could only intervene diplomatically, and the Europeans, militarily, after the one issue which they had never squarely faced was resolved for them by the Serbs: the fate of Srebrenica. Only when the sticky issue of condoning ethnic cleansing had been removed by the parties themselves could the United States invite them to sit around the negotiating table in Dayton.

NOTES

1. Lindsey Hilsum, 'A village tyrant spells out his dream for the Serbs', *Independent*, 16 June 1996.
2. Quoted in Norman Cigar, *Genocide in Bosnia*, p. 98.
3. Impeding the men's escape is a less likely rationale, because the victims were not ordered to take their shoes off immediately after capture, but only shortly before their execution.
4. Quoted in *OMRI Special Report: Pursuing Balkan Peace*, Vol. 1, No. 11 (19 March 1996).
5. There have been suggestions that Orić was forbidden to return to the enclave by the Bosnian government. Some claim this as a sign that they had struck a secret deal with Milošević to let the enclave go. The Bosnian government either did not want to lose one of their best officers or it did not want a real, long-drawn-out struggle over the enclave. True or not, it is unlikely that the presence or absence of Orić would have made more than a marginal difference to the outcome.
6. Thirty to seventy mortars versus twenty to thirty for the Bosnian Serbs, according to a press briefing by a 'Senior DoD Official' on 11 July 1995.
7. *Dutchbat in Vredesnaam*, p. 303; see also p. 319.
8. The French quickly withdrew from the main western enclave of Bihać. The British did eventually commit troops to Goražde in spring 1994, but this was a decision by the UN commander in Bosnia, General Sir Michael Rose. He felt he could not possibly expect countries to offer troops for the safe areas if there were no British troops in any of them. Also, Goražde was the most easily defensible of the eastern enclaves and had a substantial

Bosnian army presence. The Ukrainians took on Žepa and sent some troops to Goražde as well.

9. Yasushi Akashi, 'The limits of UN diplomacy and the future of conflict mediation', *Survival*, Vol. 37, no. 4 (Winter 1995–6), p. 96.

10. Although to be fair to Defence Minister Voorhoeve, he did propose to the Bosnian government on 13 June 1995 the evacuation of the civilian population from Srebrenica together with Dutchbat. The Bosnian government, in the person of Foreign Minister Mohammed Šaćirbey, refused because 'the isolated "safe areas" were closely connected with the ideal of a multi-ethnic Bosnia-Herzegovina'.

11. Air attacks, which the Clinton administration so favoured and executed, proved relatively ineffective in September 1995. The NATO air forces quickly ran out of targets and, in 750 attack missions, bombed the same fifty-six ground targets over and over again. The Serbs were not so susceptible to air power because their 'pain barrier' had risen after they had achieved their territorial objectives in eastern Bosnia. By this stage, they could cope with air strikes by sitting tight. It was the other ground operations – by the Croats, Bosnians and RRF – that forced them to seek an end to the war.

Index